What Others Say About Doug Giles

Not all devotionals are made equal. Most of them cover the same ground with some of the same spiritual advice. That's not bad unless it's a squishy devotional that does not connect the reader to the world that wars against Christians. Some of this warfare can have deadly consequences. The religious leaders schemed to get Jesus killed using the Roman government as their tool. King Herod had James the brother of John "put to death with a sword" (Acts 12:2). Before him it was Stephen (7:54-60). Peter would die a martyr's death (John 21:18-19). John was a "fellow-partaker in the tribulation" (Rev. 1:9). Paul was beaten, stoned, and left for dead (2 Cor. 11:23-27; Acts 14:19). He knew the plight of his faithful ancestors and how they relied on God's Word for spiritual sustenance in crisis mode. We've had it easy in the United States. Those days could end. Are we mentally and biblically prepared? The Wildman Devotional: A 50-day Devotional for Men by Doug Giles is the devotional with biblical teeth. It's a guide for the daily ups and downs of life as well as a preparation handbook for what could be coming. Get it, read it, live it!

Gary DeMar
President of American Vision

"There're those men of the cloth that cater to mediocrity. There are those timid preachers that are straight up cowards, tucking their tails to the truth. Then there's those very few warriors. Doug defines that word. He's a "Spec-Ops guy" in the Kingdom of God. A true David looking for "five smooth stones."

LTC (Ret.) Pete Chambers
Green Beret, Special Operations Flight Surgeon

"There is NO way to describe Doug Giles adequately, so I won't even try. Suffice it to say there is NO ONE like him and I'm grateful for him!"

– Eric Metaxas

"Doug Giles speaks the truth ... he's a societal watchdog ... a funny bastard."

– Ted Nugent

"Doug Giles is a good man, and his bambinas are fearless. His girls Hannah and Regis Giles are indefatigable. I admire the Giles clan from afar."

– Dennis Miller

"Doug Giles, the perfect dynamite needed to ignite a fire in the belly of every man, woman and child to live like warriors."

– Lieutenant Colonel Allen B. West

"Doug is a Wild Man. Read his devotional."

Matt Crouch,
President, Trinity Broadcasting Network

Copyright 2022, Doug Giles, All Rights Reserved
No part of this book may be reproduced, stored in a retrieval system, or transmitted by any means without the written permission of the author.
Published by White Feather Press.
(www.whitefeatherpress.com)
Edited by Karen Walker.
ISBN 978-1-61808-214-5
Printed in the United States of America
Cover design by David Bugnon and mobopolis.com
Scriptures marked KJV are taken from the KING JAMES VERSION (KJV): KING JAMES VERSION, public domain.
Scriptures marked TM are taken from the THE MESSAGE: THE BIBLE IN CONTEMPORARY ENGLISH (TM): Scripture taken from THE MESSAGE: THE BIBLE IN CONTEMPORARY ENGLISH, copyright©1993, 1994, 1995, 1996, 2000, 2001, 2002. Used by permission of NavPress Publishing Group
"Scripture marked NASB taken from the NEW AMERICAN STANDARD BIBLE(r), Copyright (c) 1960,1962,1963,1968,1971,1972,1973,1975,1977 by The Lockman Foundation. Used by permission. https://www.lockman.org."
Scriptures marked AMP are taken from the Amplified Bible(R)
Copyright (c) 1954, 1958, 1962, 1964, 1965, 1987 by
The Lockman Foundation, La Habra, CA 90631
All rights reserved. https://www.lockman.org
Scripture quotations marked (NIV) are taken from the Holy Bible, New International Version®, NIV®. Copyright © 1973, 1978, 1984, 2011 by Biblica, Inc.™ Used by permission of Zondervan. All rights reserved worldwide. www.zondervan.com. The "NIV" and "New International Version" are trademarks registered in the United States Patent and Trademark Office by Biblica, Inc.™
Scripture quotations marked (TLB) are taken from The Living Bible, copyright © 1971 by Tyndale House Foundation. Used by permission of Tyndale House Publishers, Carol Stream, Illinois 60188. All rights reserved.
Scripture quotations marked (EXB) are taken from THE EXPANDED BIBLE. Copyright© 2011 by Thomas Nelson, Inc. Used by permission. All rights reserved.
Scriptures marked VOICE are taken from The Voice Bible Copyright © 2012 Thomas Nelson, Inc. The Voice™ translation © 2012 Ecclesia Bible Society All rights reserved.
Scripture marked NKJV taken from the New King James Version®. Copyright © 1982 by Thomas Nelson. Used by permission. All rights reserved.

The Wildman Devotional

A 50-day Devotional for Men

By Doug Giles

Dedication

This book is dedicated to my grandkids. May you forever stay bold, wild and free before our awesome God.

About the Art

The art work contained in these pages was painted by yours truly. Some originals, herein, are still available. All of these images are available as Open Edition Prints that can be customized to fit your wall space. We print on museum quality canvas, luster paper, wood and for all you metal-heads, we also print on metal. We use only the best inks in our printing process. To see these pieces and more go to Doug-Giles.Art.

Table of Contents

Introduction: What's Up With The Title?

THE WEALTH
This Confession Will Light Wet Wood 1
My Father Goes Into Action When This
Happens 5
A Prisoner Of Hope 9
If Your Christianity Is Boring, You're Doing
It All Wrong 13
Like A Narc At A Biker Party 17
Bold As A Lion 21
If You Want To Bless Your Kids … Do This 25
From A Nobody To A Somebody 29
Dos And Don'ts vs The Power Of The Holy Spirit ... 33
More Than Conquerors 39
Arise, O Lord … Save Me, O My God 43
The Seeing Eye And The Hearing Ear 47
The Power Of The Tongue 51
I Will Restore To You The Years 55
Unto Thee, O Lord, Do I Lift Up My Soul … 59
I Will Never Forsake You 63

THE WALK
Their God Is Their Belly 67
Does Christ Go Strolling With The Devil? 71
Psalm Talkin' 75
Blessings & Cursings: Max Jukes vs
Jonathan Edwards 79
Eat The Scroll 85
Four Sure Fire Ways To Ruin Your Life 89
Honor Your Father & Mother 93
Honor Your Spiritual Authority 97
Four Signs Of A Great Church 101
Are You Backslidden? 105

Young Warriors 109
Let My People Go 113
Bring The Books 117
Bring The Books - Part 2 121
Bring The Books - Part 3 125

THE WARFARE
Hast Thou No Scar? 129
Trial … You're A Friend
Of Mine 133
Holy Adrenaline 139
Welcome To The Jungle 143
Satan Presents The Bait And Hides The Hook 147
My Letter To The Devil 151
When Demons Try To Get You Down … Do This 155
How To Quick Start Your Sad, Little Life 159
How To Quick Start Your Sad, Little Life - Part 2 163
How To Quick Start Your Sad, Little Life - The Finale .. 167
Holy War 171
Stand Firm 175
Productive In Prison 179
You Can't "Love Jesus" And Not Feast On His Word ... 183
Revival From The Pit 187
Who's Training You? 191
Rider On A White Horse 195
Spiritual Violence 201
My Testimony 207

Introduction: What's Up With The Title?

Most of the current and popular Christian devotionals that I've read, even "for men", have left me more disappointed than my buddy who just found out that his Instagram crush was a guy dressed like a girl.

A devotional for dudes must have grist for the warriors' mill within its pages, from soup to nuts. It must fuel their warrior and wildman spirit that's been starved to death in the oh-so-sassy evangelical world of squishiness (Amos 8:11).

And that, my brothers, is what I've attempted to do with this fresh tome, *The Wildman Devotional: A 50-Day Devotional for Men.*

My goal herein is twofold: I'm here to put brains (Rom 12:1-2) and balls (Prov 28:1) on believers. It's my calling. It's my gifting. It's what I do 24/7/365. Yep, it's my full-time job.

If the Church is going to reach the lost, disciple the converted, leaven culture, and rebuke the political putrid swamp rats inside the Beltway and beyond then we're going to need men with *cojones* who've shored up their cranium with the Christian worldview. Can you dig it? I knew you could.

Now, I'm sure some Lysol-disinfected Christian is pearl-clutching over my usage of the word *Wildman* because they've gotten used to what Satan has sold Christendom, namely, a *Mild-man*. Well, allow me, my fragile friend, to explain what I mean by a biblical Wildman because I'm not cheerleading for some out-of-control cat who's crazier than Kamala Harris's margin doodles. Oh, no *senorita*. Here's my definition of a Wildman …

1. A Wildman is a threat to any group, party, person, or thing that attempts to keep him in a state of puerile domesticity; a veritable stooge of the machine.

2. A Wildman is a person who is free from politically correct pressure to conform to what "they, them, and the other guy" tell them to conform to or else they'll be canceled.

3. A Wildman is unowned, unmanipulated, unbowed, unbeholden, undomesticated, unapologetic, and unashamed of who they are in God and Christ.

Y'know … just like Abraham, Moses, David, Joshua, Samson, Amos, Elijah, Nehemiah, John the Baptist, Peter, Paul, and Jesus?

Jesus wasn't manageable. He didn't give two flips about what men thought. He wasn't spooked by Satan's threats. He didn't kiss religious or political butt.

Jesus was bold, free, and wild before the Father in the epic righteous sense of the word, and you and I should take our cue from the 30-year-old Rebel from Galilee and not castrated Christendom. Can I get a witness?

To feed and fuel the Wildman spirit within you my brothers, I've divided up the diet herein to cover three spiritual food groups: 1. The Wealth; 2. The Walk; and 3. The Warfare of the Christian.

The Wealth entries showcase to the Christian how spiritually rich we are in Christ (Eph 1:1-23).

The Walk aspects herein show the believer how following Him will cause us to walk against the grain of this fetid milieu (Eph 4:1-32).

The Warfare additions prep the Christ enthusiast with weapons, armor, and attitude to wax the powers of darkness (Eph 6:10-20).

As you'll soon see, each of my devotional delicacies are short, punchy and to the point. They are not long treatises, but quick adrenaline jolts to deliver Holy Ghost food to the hungry Wildman. If you meditate throughout the day on what each entry delivered, I'm convinced you will morph into a lethal weapon that the powers of darkness will loathe to mess with.

I hope you enjoy *The Wildman Devotional: A 50-Day Devotional for Men*. If it delivered the goods to your soul, consider buying five extra copies for your buddies and have them digest this devotional as well. We need to create an army of Wildmen.

Thanks, enjoy, and stay rowdy,

Doug Giles
Somewhere in Texas

The Wealth

Day 1

This Confession Will Light Wet Wood

I've personalized this confession, for the believer, from Paul's first chapter of his letter to the Ephesians (Eph 1:1-23) using The Message translation. This is to be read out loud, with testicular fortitude, especially if you're feeling a wee bit crappy today. Enjoy and let 'er rip. You're welcome.

I, _____ (add your name), am under God's plan as a _____ (add your calling), I'm a special agent of Christ Jesus.

Grace and peace have been poured into my life by God our Father and our Master, Jesus Christ.

How blessed is God! And what a blessing you are, Lord!

You are the Father of our Master, Jesus Christ, and you take me to the high places of blessing in Him.

Long before He laid down Earth's foundations, He had me in mind, had settled on me as the focus of His love, to be made whole and holy by His love.

Long, long ago, He decided to adopt me into His family through Jesus Christ. (What pleasure He took in planning this!) He wanted me to enter into the celebration of His lavish gift-giving by the hand of His beloved Son.

Because of the sacrifice of the Messiah, His blood poured out on the altar of the Cross, I'm a free person, free of penalties and punishments chalked up by all my misdeeds. And not just barely free, either. *Abundantly* free!

He thought of everything, provided for everything I could possibly need, letting me in on the plans He took such delight in making.

He set it all out before us in Christ, a long-range plan in which everything would be brought together and summed up in Him, everything in deepest heaven, everything on planet earth. It's in Christ that I find out who I am and what I am living for.

Long before I first heard of Christ and got my hopes up, He had His eye on me, had designs on me for glorious living, part of the overall purpose He is working out in everything and everyone.

It's in Christ that once I heard the truth and believed it (this Message of my salvation), found myself home free – signed, sealed, and delivered by the Holy Spirit.

This down payment from God is the first installment on what's coming, a reminder that I'll get everything God has planned for me, a praising and glorious life.

I ask – ask the God of our Master, Jesus Christ, the God of glory – to make me intelligent and discerning in knowing Him personally, my eyes focused and clear, so that I can see exactly what it is He is calling me to do, grasp the immensity of this glorious way of life He has for his me, oh, the utter extravagance of His work for those who trust Him – endless energy, boundless strength!

All this energy issues from Christ: God raised Him from death and set Him on a throne in deep heaven, in charge of running the universe, everything from galaxies to governments, no name and no power exempt from His rule.

And not just for the time being, but *forever*. He is in charge of it all, has the final word on everything. At the center of all this, Christ rules the church. The church, you see, is not peripheral to the world; the world is peripheral to the church. The church is Christ's body, in which He speaks and acts, by which He fills everything with His presence.

Day 2

My Father Goes Into Action When This Happens

"When two of you get together on anything at all on earth and make a prayer of it, my Father in heaven goes into action."

– Matthew 18:19 (MSG)

That's a powerful little proclamation, right there my brothers.

It's kinda stupefying to me that The Son of The Living God, who sports all power and all authority in heaven and on earth, said if two of us chuckleheads get together on anything at all on earth and make a prayer of it, God the Father will go into action.

Good Lawd! What a promise, eh?

I'm sure some unsanctified goober's thinking right now, "Well, if that's true man, I want God to give me Shaniqua, my favorite stripper down at Tootsie's, to be my forever ever ever love."

Uh, earth to Dilbert, I don't think that's what is entailed in that scripture. Matter of fact, I'm pretty certain it is not what the Son of God had in mind.

Check out how the Amplified Bible frames that magnificent promise …

"Again I say to you, that if two believers on earth agree [that is, are of one mind, in harmony] about anything that they ask [within the will of God], it will be done for them by My Father in heaven."

Did you catch the distinction within that *carte blanche* via The Amplified translation? If you missed it, let me help you. It says whatsoever you ask has to be "within the will of God" before He, God, kicks into gear to get it for you. I doubt Shaniqua The Stripper falls into that parameter.

That said, there's a whole glut of holy goodies that our Heavenly Father would love to drop on our lap.

For instance …

- If you're a 10th-degree horndog enslaved to lust, He'd love to set you free from your crotchal command center and be liberated to follow that which has eternal, noble worth (Jn 8:36).

- If you're a terrified quail, He'd love to turn

The Wildman Devotional

you into a righteous bold lion (Prov 28:1)

- If you're someone who regularly spews lies, hype, and spin, He'd love to morph you into a sober truth-teller devoid of political correctness (Acts 5:29).

- If you're more confused with your existence than a termite in a yo-yo, He'd love to communicate to you your peculiar purpose while you schlep this blue pinball (Eph 1:18).

God is a righteous request-answering God. Take Jesus at His word, like a simple child, grab a buddy and do the following and see what happens …

> *"When two of you get together on anything at all on earth and make a prayer of it, my Father in heaven goes into action."*
>
> – Matthew 18:19 (MSG)

I'd love to hear how The Father fulfilled this verse in your life. Drop me an email with your testimony about how the Lord moved mightily when you prayed the prayer of agreement.

Day 3

A Prisoner Of Hope

"Return to the stronghold, O prisoners who have the hope; This very day I am declaring that I will restore double to you."

– Zechariah 9:12 (NASB)

Before I was captured by Christ at the age of twenty-one, I was a prisoner to my base, lower-cortex monkey-brain delights and pretty much all the garbage that Satan had to offer this side of an eternal hell.

When Christians were treating their body like it was a temple, I was treating mine like it was an amusement park. It was great hellish fun ... for a while at least (Eccl 8:11-13, Heb 11:24-27).

Yep, I was feelin' no pain until the Holy Spirit started convicting me of my sin, exposing my unrighteousness, and waking me up to my upcoming everlasting damnation (Jn 16:8).

It was at this juncture that I came to realize what I thought I had control over, I was now a prisoner to – namely my sin and Satan's devices (Rom 7:21-24). Indeed, a "good ol' boy" from West Texas was a veritable slave to the powers of darkness (Rom 6:16). It was a prison of my own choosing and making, and I had no one to blame except myself (Eph 2:1-10).

That's when I called out to God to …

1. Set me free from this evil bullcrap I was mired in (Ps 40:2)

2. Forgive me of all my truly wretched deeds (Ps 25:18)

3. Grant me a fresh start with Him (2Cor 5:17).

That was way back in 1983 and you know what? Christ came in like a champion and set me free from deep, enslaving strongholds. I am forever grateful for His lovingkindness and tremendous mercy because I sure as heck did not deserve one iota of His great love (Ps 103:1-5).

A famous refrain from an ancient Bob Dylan tune says, "You're gonna have to serve somebody. It may be the devil or it may be the Lord. But you're gonna have to serve somebody". As goofy as I still am and as imperfect as my walk with Christ has been, I'm giddy that I've moved from being a slave of vice and devils to being a graced and freed adopted son of the

The Wildman Devotional

Living God (Rom 6:19).

If you too are bound up by demonic forces, call out to Him today and become His prisoner of hope versus *el Diablo's* prisoner of hell. You won't regret that prayer request.

Day 4

If Your Christianity Is Boring, You're Doing It All Wrong

" Blessed be the God and Father of our Lord Jesus Christ, who has blessed us with every spiritual blessing in the heavenly places in Christ."

– Ephesians 1:3 (NASB)

I'll never forget talking to this dude in Florida who was one of the most lost and arrogant people I've ever met in my 59 trips around the sun. It was truly stupefying. He was homeless, jobless, and toothless. He had bounced in and out of jail and yet, he said Christianity is for cripples and losers and that he'd "tried Jesus" and Jesus made no difference in his life. To wit, I laughed out loud. I don't know what he "tried" but it was not the Resurrected Son of the Most

High God who reigns as King of Kings and Lord of Lords.

Contrary to that wizard, Paul says the Christian, in Christ, is insanely blessed and radically altered leaving the redeemed person far from being a crippled loser. Matter of fact, the apostle states in just a few verses in Eph 1:3-13 that the believer is …

1. Blessed with every spiritual blessing in the heavenly places in Christ.//
2. Chosen, by God, from the foundation of the world.
3. Predestined to adoption as sons and daughters through Jesus Christ to Himself, according to the good pleasure of His will.
4. Favored and lavished upon with God's grace.
5. Redeemed through His blood and forgiven of all wrongdoings.
6. Sealed with the Holy Spirit of promise. By the way, that's the same Spirit that raised Christ from the dead. Can you say, "Boom?"

Therefore, dear Christian, you are an extremely blessed dude or dudette. You're far from being a po' crippled loser. You're a veritable spiritually rich

The Wildman Devotional

demon-threatening machine that's loved by the Godhead, empowered by The Holy Spirit, with an epic purpose here on earth and in eternity to boot. If your Christianity is boring, you're doing it all wrong.

Day 5

Like A Narc At A Biker Party

"... God raised him (Jesus) from death and set him on a throne in deep heaven, in charge of running the universe, everything from galaxies to governments, no name and no power exempt from his rule. And not just for the time being, but forever. He is in charge of it all, has the final word on everything. At the center of all this, Christ rules the church. The church, you see, is not peripheral to the world; the world is peripheral to the church. The church is Christ's body, in which he speaks and acts, by which he fills everything with his presence."

– Ephesians 1:20-23 (MSG)

Next time some fear-laden hamster tells you about "the power of the Devil" and how Satan controls this world, show them this chunk of scripture. It's pretty clear to this public-school graduate that Jesus is running the show, not Satan. Hello.

Satan's a defeated created being with ⅓ of the fallen angelic hosts at his disposal (Heb 2:14).

Jesus is the resurrected Lord of Glory who has all power, all might, and all authority and has ⅔ of the angelic armies at His beck and call (Mt 28:18-20; Heb 1:7,14).

This is easy math, folks. Someone with three teeth and an IQ of 50 can understand from the aforementioned text that Christ reigns supreme both in time and in eternity.

This means, dear Christian, that you're not a victim (Rom 8:37).

You're not some doormat for the powers of darkness.

Matter of fact, he's to be your doormat (Rom 16:19,20).

It's not God's will for the world to go to hell. It is His will that Satan's devices in your life and in this country and around this blue marble get stomped like a narc at a biker party (Rev 12:7-12).

Day 6

Bold As A Lion

*"The wicked flee when no one is pursuing,
But the righteous are bold as a lion."*

– Proverbs 28:1 (NASB)

Solomon says that boldness is the trait of the righteous and the redeemed and fleeing is the trait of the wicked and the damned.

Here's a little interesting observation: You don't see Jesus fleeing when pursued by religious or political idiots or even Satan himself (Mk 1:13; Mt 23). Matter of fact, and far from fleeing, Jesus regularly got up in their grill when they went full retard in His presence.

Same thing with John the Baptist. He wasn't characterized by sporting shriveled testicles and chewing his fingernails. John was bold (Mt 11:7).

The same goes for the apostles and prophets. They were bold, salty dawgs (Acts 4:13; Acts 4:29).

Indeed, the biblical protagonists, lauded by Holy Writ, were bold before men and devils (Heb 11:1-40). They were bold in their risk-taking (Heb 11:8). They were bold in their love towards the unlovely (1Cor 1:26-31). They were bold in the faith (Heb 11:24-27). They were bold in their prayers (Acts 4:29).

They were bold with their sense of humor. Especially Elijah and Paul (1Kgs 18:27; 1Cor 4:8). Even in a culture that wanted to cancel them. Speaking of a sense of humor, comedian John Cleese of Monty Python fame, said, "Humor by its very nature is critical. And if you say there's a 'special' group of folks you can't offend then humor is gone and with humor goes a sense of proportion. And when that vanishes, as far as I'm concerned, you're living in 1984."

Yep, the biblical mainstays embodied what Daniel 11:32 says, … *"the people who know their God will be strong and take action."*

So, in case you're not getting it: the evil are the fear-laden and craven backward-looking hamsters and the true Christian is B-O-L-D, bold.

What a gift from God. The power to live bold, wild, and free in Him!

Day 7

If You Want To Bless Your Kids ... Do This

"A righteous person who walks in his integrity – How blessed are his sons after him."

– Proverbs 20:7 (NASB)

When's the last time you heard a sermon on integrity? I hear sermons all the time on miracles, faith, God's blessings, prosperity, and healing, which are all well and good, but I don't hear diddly-squat so much about walking in integrity.

Solomon says the righteous dude who walks in integrity has a massive impact on his kids and that impact is a blessing.

Check it out: If you walk in integrity your kids are going to be blessed. Blessed means in the original language that they're happy, fortunate, prosperous, and enviable. That beats the crap out of your kids being sad, cursed, broke, and despicable, eh?

For those not hip to what integrity is, integrity is the practice of being honest and showing a consistent and uncompromising adherence to strong moral and ethical principles and values. In ethics, integrity is regarded as the honesty and truthfulness or accuracy of one's actions. In other words, you walk wholeheartedly before God and you don't screw people over.

What a great legacy and an example we leave for our kids by walking in integrity before God and man. If you've blown your Christian example, just repent. God forgives. We all have done it to one extent or another. Set your compass now on true North and ask the Holy Spirit each day to make you a man of integrity. Remember that your integrity equates a massive, Holy Ghost blessing upon your kids and who would not want that?

Day 8

From A Nobody To A Somebody

"God made something out of Abraham when he was a nobody."

— Romans 4:17 (MSG)

God loves jacking with people's heads. Especially do-gooder, self-righteous, look at me I'm Sandra Dee, type of religious mooks. One of the ways He baffles their biases is by choosing and using people they don't give two flying craps about. I'm talkin' about folks the religious hoity-toity deemed unusable and unlovable. The theme of God choosing and using the base and the corrupt is so thick through scripture even Stevie Wonder can see it (1Cor 1:26-31).

Doug Giles

When God went looking for someone to become the father of many nations, He didn't go shopping for some virile Jason Momoa stud who was married to a voluptuous Italian bird with good child-bearing hips. Oh, no. He went in the exact opposite direction. He shopped where the natural mind and the religious mind would never ever consider.

Indeed, when God decided to populate the planet with His people, He picked an old dude whose wedding tackle had stopped working many, many moons ago. He also made certain that the wife Abraham was married to had no chance in hell of ever getting pregnant. Yep, God spawned a nation through an impotent hundred-year-old Iraqi cat and via the dry and dusty womb of his ninety-year-old skeptical bride.

Look man, if you feel powerless, impotent, overlooked, unlikable, dumb, too young, too old, a veritable human reject who's deemed least likely to succeed, then I have some advice for you: go pack your bag because you are going places with God because you are the exact type of person God loves to choose and use. Don't let the devil, dumb religious dorks, or your own whirring tin brain tell you otherwise.

Day 9

Dos And Don'ts vs The Power Of The Holy Spirit

"But if the Spirit of Him who raised Jesus from the dead dwells in you, He who raised Christ Jesus from the dead will also give life to your mortal bodies through His Spirit who dwells in you."

– Romans 8:11 (NASB)

Christianity has been deduced down to a bunch of life-choking religious dos and don'ts in a lot of Churches (Mk 7:4).

Here's some of the don'ts: Don't smoke cigarettes. Don't sleep with pirate hookers. Don't drink *Tito's*. Don't watch Netflix. Don't watch Fox News any more except for Tucker Carlson's show. Don't have any fun. Don't have any adventure (Col 2:21).

Some of the dos include: Do come to our predictably boring church services and do pretend that you like it. Do give us your money so that we can bore more people on a grander scale. Do dress like us. Do talk like us. Do give up your personality and your personal pizzazz and morph into a religious clone of our particular denomination. And lastly, do excuse gluttony while condemning those who have a bottle of beer or a glass of wine (Mt 23:1-5).

It's sad and sinful that pastors and Christians have taken the Greatest Story Ever Told and made it suck (2Tim 3:5).

True Christianity has jack squat to do with that religious rubbish. True Christianity is about formerly sin-loving, demon-channeling, God-denying, and sin-addled chuckleheads having Christ deliver us by His shed blood from evil spirits and filling us with the Holy Ghost (Eph 2:1-10). By the way, that's the same Spirit that raised Jesus's three-day-old corpse from the dead.

When the Holy Spirit indwells us, He spawns not odious oppressive religious rules and regulations but epic fruits and gifts. Here are the fruits of the Spirit He manifests in the believers' life:

1. Love

2. Joy

3. Peace

The Wildman Devotional

    4. Longsuffering

    5. Kindness

    6. Goodness

    7. Faithfulness

    8. Gentleness

    9. Self-control (Gal 5:22-23)

Not only does He morph us from the inside out with holy character traits that are uncommon to our carnal man, He also dumps on the believer supernatural spiritual gifts that help the Godhead expand their kingdom and wipe out Satan. Check out the spiritual gifts that Paul says the Christian can be blessed with via the Holy Spirit:

    1. The Word of Knowledge

    2. The Word of Wisdom

    3. The Gift of Prophecy

    4. The Gift of Faith

    5. The Gifts of Healings

    6. The Working of Miracles

    7. The Discerning of Spirits

    8. Different Kinds of Tongues

9. The Interpretation of Tongues (1Cor 12&14)

Ask God today to hit you with His hell-shaking spiritual gifts. Allow the Holy Spirit to kill the foul fruits of the flesh in your life and replace them with His glorious fruits of the Spirit. Those two functions of the Third Person of the Godhead beats the heck out of dead religious rules and regulations.

Day 10

More Than Conquerors

"So, what do you think? With God on our side like this, how can we lose? If God didn't hesitate to put everything on the line for us, embracing our condition and exposing himself to the worst by sending his own Son, is there anything else he wouldn't gladly and freely do for us?"

– Romans 8:31-32 (MSG)

Comedian Bill Burr said the message he received from churchy people when he was growing up in Beantown was that "God hates me and I owe Him money." A stack of Christians and unwashed heathens think that's pretty much the gospel story, namely, God's always ticked off at us and He doesn't like us that much.

Contrary to that satanic crapola, the scripture uniformly states that God radically loves radically corrupt critters like us (Rom 5:6-11).

Uh ... earth to gloomy Christian and sinners: God sent His only begotten Son to pay the ultimate penalty for our evil deeds. I'm pretty certain ... correction ... I'm very certain that is THE definition of love, not hate (Jn 3:16).

Christians who operate on feelings say stupid stuff like, "I don't feel like God loves me. I haven't felt His love in such a long time." To wit I reply, so what? Feelings are great but they're not the determining factor regarding whether or not God loves you, buttercup. When the Christian "doesn't feel the love of God" they can fall back on the empirical evidence of the incarnation of Christ, His attesting miracles, and His death, burial, resurrection, and ascension. Hello.

God put His Son on the line for us (Jn 3:16).

Embraced our demonic, sin-laden condition (1Pet 2:24).

Paid the penalty for our total depravity on the cross (Col 2:14).

Openly defeated death, hell, the grave, and the Devil (Heb 2:14).

Which led Paul to the conclusion that God greatly loves sinners, He is on our side, as in big time, so ... how can we lose?

If God was so extravagant in His love toward us when we didn't give a rat's backside about Him, shall

The Wildman Devotional

He not, gladly and freely, give us all things that pertain to life and godliness (2Pet 1:2-4)?

The short answer is … yes.

That's why Paul deduced that if God went to all that trouble when we hated Him (Eph 2:1-10) then that means, in life, we will overwhelmingly conquer whatever slop Satan sends our way (Rom 8:37-39).

Can I get a big, "Amen?"

Day 11

Arise, O Lord ... Save Me, O My God

> *"I will not be afraid of ten thousands of people Who have set themselves against me all around. Arise, Lord; save me, my God! For You have struck all my enemies on the cheek; You have shattered the teeth of the wicked. Salvation belongs to the Lord; May Your blessing be upon Your people!"*
>
> – Psalm 3:6-8

I have an old King James Bible that has an intro to this Psalm that says King David penned this poem when he was fleeing from his son Absalom who was trying to kill him. The familial hell in David's household was brought on by David himself. His adultery with Bathsheba and his successful plan to cover up his liaison with his new lady by having her husband murdered equated a holy butt whuppin' from God (2Sam 12:11) in the form of massive family problems.

Most Christians, if they screwed up so royally like David did, would probably be beset with guilt and condemnation for the rest of their days. Indeed, *el Diablo* would work them over with Linda Ronstadt's lyrics, "you're no good, you're no good, you're no good, baby you're no good" and most Christians would buy that plate of poop and ask for seconds.

David, on the other hand, truly knew God and thus knew His grace and therefore continued as God's special boy full of faith and boldness even after he had blown it badly.

Question: Have you too screwed up royally like David? If yes, don't throw away your confidence in God. David didn't and you shouldn't. Read Psalm 3 and pay attention to how David rolled after getting rolled by his demonic desires. It's pretty impressive how he bounced back from those heinous sins with his forceful faith intact.

If God helped David after his massive failure, He'll help you as well.

Day 12

The Seeing Eye And The Hearing Ear

"And the disciples came up and said to Him, 'Why do You speak to them in parables?' And Jesus answered them, 'To you it has been granted to know the mysteries of the kingdom of heaven, but to them it has not been granted. For whoever has, to him more shall be given, and he will have an abundance; but whoever does not have, even what he has shall be taken away from him. Therefore I speak to them in parables; because while seeing they do not see, and while hearing they do not hear, nor do they understand. And in their case the prophecy of Isaiah is being fulfilled, which says,

You shall keep on listening, but shall not understand; And you shall keep on looking, but shall not perceive; For the heart of this people has become dull, With their ears they scarcely hear,

And they have closed their eyes,
Otherwise they might see with their eyes,
Hear with their ears,
Understand with their heart, and return,
And I would heal them.'

But blessed are your eyes, because they see; and your ears, because they hear. For truly I say to you that many prophets and righteous people longed to see what you see, and did not see it, and to hear what you hear, and did not hear it."

— Matthew 13:10-17 (NASB)

I'd like to point out that Jesus says, in Matthew 13:10-17, that God blesses the sinner with the "seeing eye and the hearing ear."

Please note …

You don't earn the seeing eye and hearing ear with your religious good works (Rom 3:20,27).

You don't choose the seeing eye and hearing ear (Rom 3:9-18) because all a sinner chooses is darkness. Hello (Eph 2:1-10).

You don't get the seeing eye and hearing ear because you don't smoke, or listen to Katy Perry music, or drink moonshine.

If you have the ability to "see" and "hear" the special revelation contained in the Gospel and have been "born again" thereby ... Well, that came from the Godhead and it has jack squat to do with you, *amigo*. It's what the scripture calls, "a gift." A gift, by the way, that not everyone has (Rom 9:14-18).

The Wildman Devotional

My response to The Trinity for gifting me with eyes to see and ears to hear is ...

1. A big ol' thankful heart because this gross, formerly drug-addled sinner, did nothing and I mean nothing, to warrant that holy deposit (Heb 13:15).

2. It makes me want to live totally for Him, not because of the threat of hell and eternal punishment, but simply because I'm honored and gobsmacked that He would call, choose, and use a jackass like me (Rom 5:8).

3. This spurs me on to not want to squander His gift but grow in grace and the knowledge and revelation of Christ. A grace, of which, He so lavishly bestowed upon us whom He has granted the ability to see and hear (Eph 1:17-23).

4. Lastly, this gift of the "seeing eye and the hearing ear" is Good News that I want to tell to bad people because God wants multitudes of gnarly folks to hear His gracious call. The God who saves the damned does it by the means of the foolishness of preaching (1Cor 1:21) so ... let's preach!

"How then are they to call on Him in whom they have not believed? How are they to believe in Him whom they have not heard? And how are they to hear without a preacher?"

– Romans 10:14 (NASB)

Day 13

The Power Of The Tongue

"Words kill, words give life; they're either poison or fruit—you choose."

– Proverbs 18:21 (MSG)

James said in James 3:6 that we can create hell in our life by our unbridled tongue.

Conversely, Solomon says, in Proverbs 18:21, that death and life are in the power of the tongue.

Here's a question for you: What type of verbiage are you spewing over your life and your loved ones? Huh?

What are you declaring over our nation?

Are you declaring blessings or curses over your

Church, Family, and State?

When Moses sent the twelve spies into Canaan to check out the Promised Land, ten of the spies said they were like "grasshoppers before the enemy" (Num 13:33).

Yep, they said that they were wee little bugs before the badass warriors of Canaan. Guess what the ten shriveled testicle tepid spies became, little children? If you guessed they became grasshoppers then pat yourself on the back because you're correct.

They first said they were grasshoppers and then they became grasshoppers.

In contrast to those ten goobers, Joshua and Caleb said that they could whip the Canaanites' backside, and guess what? They did. And they did it at the ripe old age of 85 (Num. 14:38).

Here's the bottom line, Christian: if you think and say you can't, you won't.

If you think and say you can do all things through Christ who strengthens you, you will.

Or as Dr. Peterson put it:

"Words kill, words give life; they're either poison or fruit—you choose."

– Proverbs 18:21 (MSG)

Day 14

I Will Restore To You The Years

"And I will restore to you the years that the locust hath eaten, the cankerworm, and the caterpiller, and the palmerworm, my great army which I sent among you."

– Joel 2:25 (KJV)

The People of God, prior to when Joel penned the aforementioned verse, had been for decades blowing God off. They gave God mere lip service. They were CINOS: Christians In Name Only. Y'know … like the majority of evangelicals today? They said they loved God but their hearts were far from Him.

So, God, being the faithful Father He is, sent a

multifaceted plague of locusts to wake their haggard backsides up and boy oh, boy did that work!

The locusts stripped and devoured everything they loved and relied upon causing them to finally, in desperation, return to Jehovah.

God, being unlike most mean legalists, was happy to see them come back to their senses. He not only forgave them but declared unto them that He'll make up for the years that they lost getting devoured by locusts or in our vernacular, getting eaten alive by the bad decisions we made.

Therefore, my dear Christian, if you've lost years by following the superfluity of naughtiness; if you're backslidden, cold and indifferent to God and His great kingdom concerns; please note that He will not only forgive you but will bless you so greatly that He'll restore what hell attempted to destroy. He'll set you back up your heels in high fashion. You will not be browbeaten and despised by God.

Lastly, remember when God restores a fallen Christian it is always greater in quality, quantity, and kind. Run to Him and be watchful, zealous, humble, and wholehearted and watch God make up for those wasted years that "the locusts have eaten."

Day 15

Unto Thee, O Lord, Do I Lift Up My Soul ...

"Unto thee, O Lord, do I lift up my soul. O my God, I trust in thee: let me not be ashamed, let not mine enemies triumph over me."

– Psalm 25:1-2 (KJV)

David's getting jackhammered ... again. His soul is sagging, it's "down" according to him. There's a possibility of him being shamed and the enemy getting the best of him.

Here's an FYI for all Christians: Just because you're God's special kid doesn't mean you're going to be spared life's woodchipper. God loved David but God, in His love and wisdom, allowed David to get his ears boxed by the enemy. That's life folks. We're in a spiritual war and the enemy does enemy stuff.

Our adversary, the Devil, wants to crush your soul, embarrass you, and, ultimately, destroy you. So, what's the Christian to do when under assault? Cry? Whine? Renounce God? No. We're to take our cue from David and respond how this Shepherd/King responded.

David did the following …

1. He lifted his soul up to God. Most people when they get into a pickle start calling, texting, and chatting up everyone and anyone about their problem except the Lord. David went directly to God. Imagine that. Actually going to God first? Indeed, David didn't seek Nathan, Samuel, Jonathan, his mighty men of valor, or his eight wives' assistance. He sought God's … *"Unto to THEE, O Lord, do I lift up my soul …"*. Consequently, follow David's lead and go to God first.

2. David declared his trust in God. David didn't declare he was screwed. He didn't declare his internal fears or what the Devil had to say about his sticky situation. David knowing deeply the nature and character of his God through many, many battles forthrightly declared, *"O my God, I trust in thee."* In other words, David defied any and all fears

The Wildman Devotional

that would seek him to view God as untrustworthy and unreliable in rough circumstances.

Try those two little ditties the next time the enemy is on you like stink on a monkey and watch God rescue you like He did David.

Day 16

I Will Never Forsake You

"... I will never desert you, nor will I ever abandon you,"

– Hebrews 13:5 (NASB)

Here's some stuff they don't talk about in today's feelgood, grin until your teeth are dry, Church of The Warm and Fuzzies.

People will desert you. You will get abandoned.

Joy to the world, eh?

Here's some easy math: If people abandoned and deserted the sinless Son of God – they're going to do it to you.

Here's a few reasons why we get abandoned.

1. Maybe you suck. Sometimes people dump us because they should dump us. Hello. We can be a bad influence. We can be toxic. I've had people dump me because … well … they should have. The upshot of this hard little pill to swallow is, God can make you not suck if you follow His lead. This means listening to His rebuke and taking responsibility for your dirty deeds. In addition to that prescription, have someone hold you accountable so you don't veer off into suck zone ever again and become a person people should avoid.

2. Maybe you're a threat to them. If you're growing in God and your buddies aren't, they're not going to want to be around you because you convict them of their crappy walk with God. So, naturally, their rebellious flesh is going to run from you. The upshot of this altercation is that God'll lead you into better relationships with peeps that'll stoke that holy flame inside of you.

The cool thing about God is that when you get abandoned for either sucking or for being on fire for Christ, He will never leave you or forsake you. Therefore, when (not if) it happens, learn to rest in His arms of love. People are fickle. That's humanity. God's not fickle. He's committed to you 110% and you can take that to the bank.

The Wildman Devotional

Finally, listen to how the Amplified Bible translates Hebrews 13:5. It. Is. GOLD.

> *" ... for He [God] Himself has said, I will not in any way fail you nor give you up nor leave you without support. [I will] not, [I will] not, [I will] not in any degree leave you helpless nor forsake nor let [you] down (relax My hold on you)! [Assuredly not!]"*

THE WALK

Day 17

Their God Is Their Belly

"Brethren, be followers together of me, and mark them which walk so as ye have us for an ensample. (For many walk, of whom I have told you often, and now tell you even weeping, that they are the enemies of the cross of Christ: Whose end is destruction, whose God is their belly, and whose glory is in their shame, who mind earthly things.)"

– Philippians 3:17-19 (KJV)

Paul's not describing the general unwashed masses and their typical glide path of unbridled carnal ambitions in the passage above. No, Paul's describing so-called Christians who think they're heaven-bound for glory and yet they don't give two flibbertigibbets about dying to their flesh, sacrificing their lives, and living wholly unto God (2Tim 3:1-5).

Paul warns the Church in Philippi to steer clear of these dipsticks and follow his example of radical obedience to the call of Christ.

So, how do we recognize and avoid pseudo-saints?

Well, Paul puts forth four characteristics of these self-deceived dolts.

1. They're enemies of the cross of Christ. In a New Testament sense this means: A) They think their "good works" save and/or add to their salvation and not salvation by faith alone in Jesus' finished work on the cross and the imputation of His righteousness to the sinner (Eph 2:1-10). B) You can also be an enemy of the cross of Christ when all you want to do is live on Easy Street and not die to your flesh and fully follow Him (Mt 10:28-41).

2. Their God is their belly. In our parlance, the "belly" means worldly appetites, unbridled sensuality, and a peacock-like pursuit of vanity. Y'know … pretty much all the crap you see goes down in American evangelicalism nowadays (1Jn 2:15-17).

3. They glory in their shame. Essentially, these fake folks are proud of what they should be ashamed of. If you need an example of this just logon to Instagram (Ezek 16:49).

4. They mind earthly things. These *faux* believers are fixated with fleshly pleasures and are allergic to godly duty (2Tim 3:4).

The Wildman Devotional

Paul says to do yourself and God a favor and flee from these religious jackanapes because they're heading for destruction.

Day 18

Does Christ Go Strolling With The Devil?

"Don't become partners with those who reject God. How can you make a partnership out of right and wrong? That's not partnership; that's war. Is light best friends with dark? Does Christ go strolling with the Devil?"

– 2 Corinthians 6:14-15 (MSG)

I've heard Pastors say, "It doesn't matter who a Christian votes for or what political party they support. We're just called to love Jesus." Uh, sorry *senorita*. That's spiritual-sounding *stercore tauri*.

I think it does matter. If a political party is cool with …

1. Murdering unborn babies (Hos 13:16; Ez 23:29).

2. Same-sex marriage (Rom 1:18-28; Mt 19:3-6).

3. Teaching 5–9-year-olds that sodomy and transgenderism is groovy (Lk 17:1-2).

4. Declaring only white people are pure evil when everyone, outside of Christ, is radically corrupt (Rom 3:9-18).

5. Bowing to godless foreign countries that hate America (Ez 28:9).

6. Allowing a lawless invasion of our Southern border (1Tim 1:9).

7. Being unable to define what a woman is (Gen 1:26-28).

8. Big dudes competing against smaller women in sports (Prov 20:23).

9. Forcing little children to wear ineffective face masks and take ineffective vaccines (2Jn 12).

10. Publicly booing God at their National Convention (Isa 1:4; Prov 24:24).

If a political party does the aforementioned (and supports many other anti-biblical policies) then they are officially raging against righteousness and a Christian would be sinning if they supported that garbage (Prov 4:14; Jas 4:17)

The Wildman Devotional

Governments are supposed to protect and praise what is good and punish what is evil. That's "good and evil" as defined by the word of God and not Netflix (Rom 13:1-5; 1Pet 2:13-15). When a government ceases to do that then the Christian is duty-bound not to support those less than civil magistrates (Acts 5:29).

Day 19

Psalm Talkin'

"Speaking to yourselves in psalms ..."
— Ephesians 5:19 (KJV)

The apostle Paul commands believers, by inspiration of the Holy Spirit, to speak to one another using the Psalms. Speak in Psalms. That's easy enough to understand, eh?

Please note: Paul doesn't say ...

1. Speak in Fauci.
2. Speak in CNN.
3. Speak in fear.
4. Speak in what your kooky aunt thinks.

5. Speak in your denomination or non-denomination's lingo.

6. Speak in wokeism.

7. Speak in political correctness.

8. Speak doom and gloom.

9. Speak doubt.

10. Speak about all your problems.

No, the apostle says when we gather together and open our yapper that we're to let the Psalms, or "Palms" as Biden calls them, tumble off our tongues.

So, why does Paul command Christians to quote the Psalms to each other? Well, they were written by a Holy Ghost inspired warrior poet who faced monsters, went through hell and back, and kicked major backside for God's kingdom. That's why.

God would rather hear that being discussed instead what most Christians blather about.

David had nary an ounce of, "I quit" in him (Ps 3:6).

David did not have an eschatology of defeat in his spirit (Ps 37:9).

David didn't have a low or little view of God (Ps 18:1-19).

David was into discussing God's mission versus

The Wildman Devotional

gossiping about his neighbor (Ps 2:1-12)

David was a big picture dude and not some solipsistic navel-gazing Christian dipstick (1Sam 17:45-47).

Even though David was far from perfect, God was so behind what that man penned many moons ago that He tells the church, through Paul's epistle, if you speak, speak in the Psalms.

Give it a try next time you gather together with other believers.

It might just change the world (Acts 17:6).

Day 20

Blessings & Cursings: Max Jukes vs Jonathan Edwards

"Praise the Lord. Blessed are those who fear the Lord, who find great delight in his commands. Their children will be mighty in the land; the generation of the upright will be blessed. Wealth and riches are in their houses, and their righteousness endures forever."

– Psalm 112:1-3 (NIV)

Dear Christian Dad: If you don't think seriously honoring God is important to you or your progeny then please check out what happened to Max Jukes and his cursed brood in contrast with the blessings that cascaded down upon Jonathan Edwards and his extended family. Enjoy.

In 1874, Richard Dugdale, on behalf of the New York Prison Commission began to visit state prison facilities and, in doing so, discovered a particular family connection between some of the incarcerated guests in Ulster County.

The research led to a publication of a study entitled *The Jukes: A Study in Crime, Pauperism, Disease and Heredity*.

He traced the lineage of this family tree to a man of Dutch ancestry named "Max," born in 1720 in the Hudson Valley and he wasn't a particular fan of God or raising his kids in a righteous manner and his stupid, evil devil-wife was onboard with his goofy glide-path.

Dugdale estimated that there were 1,200 members of this family tree and was able to report on the details of 540 of these descendants, plus another 169 who married into the family line.

Of the total group of related individuals, Dugdale found that:

- 310 were paupers who spent a combined 2,300 years in poorhouses;

- 130 were convicted criminals;

- 50 women were prostitutes;

- 7 were murderers.

These paupers and criminals cost the state of New York $1.5 million to pay for their incarcerations and $1.25 million in public welfare and other costs to society apart from incarceration. That's $35M+ in today's costs.

In 1900, Albert Edward Winship published another supplemental study, *Jukes-Edwards: A Study in Education and Heredity*, this time tracing the descendants of America's leading theologian, Jonathan Edwards to compare them with the Jukes family.

The results are fascinating. He reported that out of approximately 1,400 known descendants of Edwards …

- "Practically no lawbreakers";

- More than 100 lawyers and 30 judges;

- 13 college presidents, 100+ professors;

- 100 clergymen, missionaries and theological professors;

- 62 physicians;

- 80 elected public officials, including 3 mayors, 3 governors, several congressmen, 3 senators and 1 vice-president (Aaron Burr);

- 60 authors or editors with 135 books to their credit; and

- 75 army or navy officers.

You see my brethren, Jonathan Edwards built God's house so God built his house.

Max Jukes blew God's house off, so God blew his house/family off.

> *" ... for them that honour me I will honour, and they that despise me shall be lightly esteemed."*
>
> *– 1Sam 2:30 (KJV)*

Day 21

Eat The Scroll

"Then He said to me, 'Son of man, eat what you find; eat this scroll, and go, speak to the house of Israel.'"

– Ezekiel 3:1 (NASB)

When my two daughters were wee little babies, they were frickin' huge. They had massive fat rings all up and down their little torsos. They looked like the Michelin Man. Their cheeks looked like two pinkish tether balls were smashed together. It was so funny. They just loved to eat. They were big-time titty babies and it showed.

I remember asking their doctor, "Are they supposed to be this fat?" He said, "Of course. A healthy appetite is a good thing. They're doing great. When they're not hungry and they're not eating … well …

that's when you should be concerned."

Christians should have, if they're spiritually healthy, a massive hunger for the Word of God as Peter said, *"... like newborn babies, long for the pure milk of the word, so that by it you may grow in respect to salvation."* (1Pet 2:2)

One thing that has stunned me over the last thirty-nine years of following The Rebel from Galilee is biblical ignorance in evangelical circles.

Yep, a lot of "Christians" are not hungry for God's word. They want His blessings, His prosperity, His peace, His forgiveness, etc., … but they don't want to do due diligence and renew their mind via the V*erbum Dei.*

Ergo, they stay stunted and biblically unhealthy. They become these emaciated little spiritual pygmies who sound like Britney Spears when they open their mouths to discuss the things of God. Some of them read more Tony Robbins, Deepak Chopra, and Oprah than they do Matthew, Mark, Luke, and John and yet they wonder, "Why is life kicking the shiitake mushrooms out of me?" Well, Dinky … it's primarily because you're not feasting on the scripture, which conveys the wisdom and the power of God and causes the Christian to grow thereby, that's "why".

So, Dear Reader, don't be like the goofy "believer" who ignores the scripture. Be like ol' Zeke, whom I quoted for this entry, and "eat the scroll." Fill your spiritual belly with the word of God. Know it backwards and forwards and up and down. Make the

The Wildman Devotional

scripture your Book of Books. All the great men and women of God were great students of the scripture. Follow their example and not the ignoramuses who ignore the most powerful Book in the world.

Day 22

Four Sure Fire Ways To Ruin Your Life

"Blessed is the man that walketh not in the counsel of the ungodly, nor standeth in the way of sinners, nor sitteth in the seat of the scornful. But his delight is in the law of the Lord; and in his law doth he meditate day and night. And he shall be like a tree planted by the rivers of water, that bringeth forth his fruit in his season; his leaf also shall not wither; and whatsoever he doeth shall prosper."

– Psalm 1:1-3 (KJV)

Question: Do you want your life to suck worse than an airplane toilet? If you do, then do the following and do not deviate from what I'm about to counsel you. Are you ready? Are you taking notes? You are? Well, giddy up. Here we go …

1. Follow people, groups, politicians, and worldviews that hate God and embrace the exact opposite of what the Bible espouses.

2. Become soulmates with folks who're good for nothing and who imbibe deeply upon the superfluity of naughtiness.

3. Settle nicely into relationships with know-it-alls who're cynical and apathetic, who're always willing to believe the worst as long as it takes as little effort as possible.

4. Do not read the word of God and sure as heck don't meditate on its principles.

Indeed, if you do the aforementioned, you will by fiat, ensure your life will be a cursed existence.

WARNING: Failure to follow these four steps will make you God-blessed and prosperous and we wouldn't want that, eh?

You're welcome.

Day 23

Honor Your Father & Mother

"Honor your father and mother (which is the first commandment with a promise)."

– Ephesians 6:2 (NASB)

When I first got converted from being a full-fledged, honorary member, of the "This Dude Couldn't Be More Lost or Bone-headed Brigade", I used to badger my parents about giving their life to Christ.

Here I was, after twenty-one years of making their lives a living hell, now I'm telling them they needed to get their act together before God and repent of their sins.

I meant well, but I was being a religious jackass about it.

I'll never forget one day I was praying and the Lord spoke to me, via His Word, and said, "Honor your Father and Mother." I took that to mean, "Quit preaching and pestering them with my newfound faith and just be a good son and show them love and respect."

For the next few decades, that's exactly what I and my family did. I dialed down with the repent rhetoric and cranked up the honor.

My mom died at 70 and my dad passed away at 84. While they were on this blue marble, we lavished them with love and good times. My dad and I fished all the time in South Florida and hunted boar in the Everglades; we pursued deer, turkeys, and exotics throughout Texas and hunted bears up in Maine. I filmed a lot of our adventures. My family and I would throw him parties when he was with us and many times I told him how much I appreciated how he and mom never gave up on me when everybody and their dog was telling them to.

I'm happy to report that before their passing they both became believers. Sometimes I wonder if they would have converted to Christ if I'd continued to be a religious crank instead of an honoring son. I am glad the Holy Spirit got through to me with the command to "Honor your Father and Mother."

The Wildman Devotional

If you have decent folks whether they're Christians or not (or your actual parents!) give them a call today and tell them that you love them and appreciate all that they've done for you.

Day 24

Honor Your Spiritual Authority

"And now, friends, we ask you to honor those leaders who work so hard for you, who have been given the responsibility of urging and guiding you along in your obedience. Overwhelm them with appreciation and love!"

– 1Thessalonians 5:12-13 (MSG)

I love shocking people. When I was little, I used to put a rubber rattlesnake under the covers of my grandma's bed. I'd hide around the corner of her room after we all had said our "goodnights" and watch her turn the sheets down as she got ready to crash. The snake worked every time. She hated snakes and when she saw that faux reptile under the covers she'd scream and jump onto a chair which ain't bad for a 90-year-old granny.

If you'd like to shock your pastor, mentor, or teacher who has sown into you wisdom, encouragements, and exhortations that to some, have literally saved their life do this:

1. Honor them.
2. Overwhelm them with appreciation.
3. Overwhelm them with love.

That'll shock the bejesus out of them because most ministers get the exact opposite from their ungrateful, dishonoring, and the petty rabble that they pastor.

So, to freak your pastor out and dang near shock 'em to death by doing the following …

1. Tell them that they rock.
2. Tell them you're so happy God led you and yours to their church.
3. Pay them a handsome salary.
4. Shock them with giving that local body of believers your time, talent, and treasure.
5. Freak them out by not bitching and complaining all the time.
6. Blow their minds by enthusiastically saying, "Amen" while they're preaching.

The Wildman Devotional

7. Lead people to Christ and fill the church with new folks on fire for God.

8. Show up on time full of faith and the overcomers' spirit.

9. Tell them more good news about your life versus bad news.

10. Y'know ... be an asset to your pastor vs. being a jackass.

I guarantee, if you do the aforementioned, you will shock your pastor and please the Lord. Google Hebrews 13:17 if you don't believe me.

Day 25

Four Signs Of A Great Church

"They were continually devoting themselves to the apostles' teaching and to fellowship, to the breaking of bread and to prayer."

— Acts 2:42 (NASB)

When most clowns go looking for a "good church" they usually mean they're looking for the following …

1. Great "Christian" entertainment.
2. Big Screens.
3. Skinny jeans.
4. Smoke machines.
5. Great coffee.

6. A fun atmosphere.

7. Some place to dump off their demonic kids that they haven't disciplined.

8. A groovy pastor.

9. Very short services.

10. Feel-good messages that require nothing from the congregant whatsoever.

Fortunately, for the masturbatory, spiritual, me-me-me-me-monkey there's a lot of those churches here in the United States of Asininity. Hucksters have created an American gospel enterprise, a veritable hot tub religion, and it seems to be working quite well because most of those churches that employ such gimmicks are packed, baby. I said, they're packed. And you can't argue with success, we're told. Or, can you?

The Bible's pretty clear that the believer should flee that ear-tickling mess (2Tim 4:3-4).

When the primitive church exploded with growth in the first century, the Holy Spirit was oh, so kind to show us His simple formula for a "good church". Check it out …

> *"They were continually devoting themselves to the apostles' teaching and to fellowship, to the breaking of bread and to prayer."*
>
> – Acts 2:42 (NASB)

So, according to the Bible, here's what The Trinity

considered a legit gathering of the elect:

1. The Christians were devoted to the apostle's doctrine.
2. The Christians were devoted to fellowship.
3. The Christians were devoted to breaking bread.
4. The Christians were devoted to prayer.

If you're looking for a "good church", meaning a biblical one, look for a body of believers who are serious about what the apostles taught, who have great fellowship, who regularly dine together, and who pray like the third monkey trying to get on Noah's Ark.

If you can find a group of folks doing the aforementioned, I'd advise you to saddle up and ride with them because that's the kind of holy stuff the Holy Spirit births and not the other politically correct, feel-good, religious slop.

Day 26

Are You Backslidden?

"The backslider gets bored with himself; the godly man's life is exciting."

– Proverbs 14:14 (TLB)

Here are five signs, according to Chuck Finney (and paraphrased by me), that your heart is backslidden and you're drifting away from God.

1. You have a never-ending search for worldly amusements. People who are always chasing pleasures, who must fill their lives with innumerable toys and must always be playing, have been consumed – eaten up – by the world. Sure, we've got to rest and play ... no argument here. What I'm thinking about is the pleasure-monger who's addicted to fun and allergic to godly duty (2Tim 3:1-5).

2. You have a lack of enjoyment and interest in God's word. One sure sign that you're slowly absorbing too much of the world is that you are not enjoying God's presence, and your Bible is collecting dust. When the heart loves God, real communion with Him is a must. It's not a hassle (Ps 69:9).

3. You exhibit outward formality in Christian exercises. A formal way of saying and doing things, which is clearly a result of habit rather than the outflow of one's heart, is a sign of absorption. When this person sings, speaks or does anything in God's name, he does it with all the excitement of Donald Trump attending a lingerie party hosted by Nancy Pelosi (Mk 7:6).

4. You neglect church for slight reasons. I know that some churches are about as inspiring as Mitch McConnell reading Leviticus backwards in Latin after drinking six bottles of Nyquil. But you and I both know that there are a great number of Christ-centered, Bible-believing churches that are excited about God's word (Heb 10:26).

   If just one of these gatherings takes place in a home or in a building in your city, and you know about it – and you miss it for some lame reason – then you can unrest assured that you are far away from God.

5. You have lost interest in truly spiritual conversation and/or your spiritual conversation is greatly lacking in content. When it's easier and more engaging to prattle on about any – and everything on earth but God and His cause, there's something wrong. When our conversation comes to a screeching halt when the things of God are mentioned, or our depth of contribution in such conversation makes Mariah Carey sound like C.S. Lewis, we've got to ask ourselves, "What the heck has happened to me?" (Heb 5:11-14).

Day 27

Young Warriors

"Let no one look down on your youthfulness, but rather in speech, conduct, love, faith, and purity, show yourself an example of those who believe."

– 1Timothy 4:12 (NASB)

Dear Young Christian Adult: Do you realize that no matter how neglected and confused you may feel, you are the key, under the discipline of the Holy Spirit, to turn this *Titanic* of a nation around before it hits the proverbial iceberg?

The prophet Joel said it is the young men and women who will have the visions that will constructively shape our future (Joel 2:28).

That's you, Dude.

Don't think that God will never use you just because you're young. Throughout Scripture and history, youth have had an incredible influence on our society. The Scripture is replete with examples of God using – and in dramatic fashion – young men and women.

You know, when most of us think about the type of person God uses, we usually think of some old cat sporting a gray beard, wearing little eyeglasses with a scowl on his face carting around a Bible that's bigger than some big chick's panties. We forget that Jesus Himself started His ministry when He was thirty years old and was finished at the ripe old age of thirty-three. Check out this short list of young "greats" found in the Scripture and in Church history and let this motivate you to seek God in order for Him to use you in like manner.

- John the Baptist was a little over the 30-mark when he rocked all of Israel.

- David was a youth when he slew Goliath. When God sought for a man to eternally shut Goliath's pie hole, he found a youth who acted like a man.

- Solomon became king over Israel at an early age, and God gave this young king wisdom that blew away his elders.

- Jeremiah, as a youth, was called as a prophet to the nations – to uproot, destroy, build and plant them according to the word of God.

- Charles Spurgeon was only nineteen when he

The Wildman Devotional

began his acclaimed pastorate in England.

- John Calvin, at twenty-seven years of age, wrote his world-reforming Institutes, which has profoundly impacted theological and political thought.

As Benjamin Disraeli said, "The history of heroes is the history of youth." God has a high view of youth. It's not because they are cute, but because they are spiritually lethal. They are the warriors that God uses to cut a swath through the demonic bondages that hold men captive. Their zeal is proverbial ... and when it is mixed with divine wisdom, they are a severe threat to Satan and his defeated ilk.

All the aforementioned young adults were forces, and he that is destined to be a force will be put on his mettle at an early age.

So get with it, young adult. Quit being a slacker ... get a vision ... get on your face ... and get ready for God to make you the next giant slayer.

Day 28

Let My People Go

"Then the Lord said to Moses, 'Go to Pharaoh and say to him, 'Thus says the Lord, 'Let My people go, so that they may serve Me.'

– Exodus 8:1 (AMP)

Before I got converted, I thought Christianity was for wussies and guess who never dreamt of being a big ol' wussy? Uh … that would be me.

After conversion at the age of twenty-one, I dug into the word of God and found out that just because you're a Christian, it doesn't mean you have to throw out your brains and hand over your balls.

Matter of fact, God digs courageous righteous rebels against bad government and the scripture is replete with them.

Our founders, fueled by the Christian worldview, were also glorious rebels with a cause. Check out these ten ditties from Thomas Jefferson's quill. For those who like refrigerator magnets below is an epic list to decorate your fridge with. Enjoy.

1. The spirit of resistance to government is so valuable on certain occasions, that I wish it to be always kept alive. It will often be exercised when wrong, but better so than not to be exercised at all.

2. It is error alone which needs the support of government. Truth can stand by itself. Subject opinion to coercion: whom will you make your inquisitors?

3. A free people [claim] their rights as derived from the laws of nature, and not as the gift of their chief magistrate.

4. If people let the government decide what foods they eat and what medicines they take, their bodies will soon be in as sorry a state as are the souls of those who live under tyranny.

5. The multiplication of public offices, increase of expense beyond income, growth and entailment of a public debt, are indica-

tions soliciting the employment of the pruning knife.

6. And can the liberties of a nation be thought secure when we have removed their only firm basis, a conviction in the minds of the people that these liberties are the gift of God? That they are not to be violated but with his wrath? Indeed I tremble for my country when I reflect that God is just: that his justice cannot sleep forever.

7. No freeman shall be debarred the use of arms [within his own lands or tenements].

8. The principle of spending money to be paid by posterity, under the name of funding, is but swindling futurity on a large scale.

9. Laws that forbid the carrying of arms... disarm only those who are neither inclined nor determined to commit crimes... Such laws make things worse for the assaulted and better for the assailants; they serve rather to encourage than to prevent homicides, for an unarmed man may be attacked with greater confidence than an armed man.

10. I hold it that a little rebellion now and then is a good thing, and as necessary in the political world as storms in the physical .

Day 29

Bring The Books

"Bring the ... books, especially the parchments."

– 2Timothy 4:13 (NASB)

Before I became a Christian, I loathed the menial level of my literary intake. Prodigious I was not. Spending twenty-one years skating through school trying to read as little as possible because Pink Floyd told me, "We don't need no education," left me working at a gas station, smoking weed, and one audition away from *Dumb & Dumber*.

Christ had to drag me into His kingdom in order to change my view of education. His pulling me out of the miry clay not only freed me from serious iniquity, but also gave me a desire and a reason to shape up the silly putty between my ears.

Having said that, if you're feeling a wee bit daft,

here's what one can do to combat one's self-inflicted stupidity.

First of all, build a library.

Every Christian needs a killer library covering a wide variety of topics. Don't just read the things your own denomination or non-denomination peddles. You'll get warped if you feed solely within an insular environment. Here are some basic categories to get you started:

The Bible. Get one and – as odd as this sounds – read it. From stem to stern. It doesn't help you to have it on your nightstand. It's not a lucky charm, even though it is magically delicious. Read it in as many versions as possible. Make it your book of books.

Study Aids. I recommend actually purchasing a concordance, a lexicon, a standard dictionary, a thesaurus, an exhaustive Scripture reference guide, a Bible dictionary, and a Webster's 1828 dictionary. The reason being? Well, I'm old and I like actual books I can hold and write in, that's "why". Sure, you'll be out a little cash – but you're going to use them for the rest of your life. Changing the world is a costly venture. So, pay the price. That said, if you're more of an online person, then as you well know, the world is your oyster when it comes to having access to excellent info.

Theology. The other day I heard this guy say, "I don't like theology ...I just love Jesus." I replied in my usual first-Corinthians-thirteen manner: "Excuse me, Mr. Bodine, but what turnip wagon did you fall

The Wildman Devotional

off of, and which wheel ran you over?"

The fact of the matter is, you can't love God if you don't know Him biblically. The study of theology is not just a matter of orthodoxy, but one of love. Every Christian is a theologian – either a good one or a bad one.

For God's sake, your sake, the Church's sake, and the unbeliever's sake – study the Word. Study in order to make you wise unto salvation, but also to make you effective and powerful in explaining it to others – both sinners and saints, both the learned and the supermodels.

Take your faith seriously.

To be continued …

Day 30

Bring The Books - Part 2

"Bring the ... books, especially the parchments."

– 2 Timothy 4:13 (NASB)

Herewith are some additional topics to flesh out your library ...

Biographies. Read about the lives of great men and women of God who had powerful ministries, influenced godly political change, fought for human rights, fed the poor, and sacrificed everything to reach men for the glory of Christ. Read about their struggles, their failures, and their triumphs. Then follow those good ol' shampoo instructions: lather, rinse and repeat ... Apply their actions and faith and attitudes in the situation to which God has presently called you.

Books on the Martyrs. Here's some unnerving reading: the cost that a few brave hearts paid to advance the Gospel. Reading about the martyrs gives the believer a historical object lesson of the people who actually believed the Gospel and lived it out to the point that it cost them their lives. In addition to this, it gives great perspective to our problems, revealing that the great majority of what we are going through is tremendously inconsequential ... a mere molehill in the Garden of Eden.

The martyrs will shake you to the core and jerk any grumbling, complaining and lukewarm slack out of your spiritual life.

Philosophy and Philosophers. Most folks who major in philosophy in college usually end up tending bar at Chili's. Philosophy is seen by the average American to be about as useful in "real life" as a crappy gun in mud. Nevertheless, this discipline (even if it doesn't seem like an urgent imperative to know and understand) affects not only the way we think, but, just as importantly, the way we live.

Philosophy takes a closer look at the ideas behind how we live our lives. What we believe to be true affects our view of ourselves, how we treat other humans and the world in which we live. Though it doesn't seem like there is a lot of thought involved in social media, most conversations, TV, politics, and educational policy – be assured, these all stem from a system of thought. As believers, we must recognize these thought systems in order to first deconstruct the destructive components in them that lead to the demise of our culture and then reconstruct a more excellent way according to God's wisdom.

The Wildman Devotional

Studying philosophy is a must, as it helps the young Christian to recognize what is really being said, where the ideas come from, and where they are going to lead.

History. Those who don't learn from the past are doomed to repeat it. If you don't believe me, just ask Amber Heard.

There is much to be learned by pausing to look backward and then chilling out and thinking about what has transpired up until now. When one studies history, one quickly begins to see the prosperity of nations that honored God and the dissolution of those who turned their backs on Him. Studying our past gives us discernment for our present decisions and wisdom in our plans for tomorrow.

Day 31

Bring The Books - Part 3

"Bring the ... books, especially the parchments."

– 2Timothy 4:13 (NASB)

And lastly, here's the last category I recommend for you to purchase in order to further flesh out your fledgling library.

The Classics. Because today's youth have the concentration level of a whitetail deer on crystal meth, a working vocabulary below that of Snoop Dog's Macaw, the passion of Britney Spears wanting to answer the ultimate questions of life, and a total IQ less than the front row of a Travis Scott concert – the Classics today stand even more neglected than Rosie's *8 Minute Abs* download.

According to Os Guinness, when most people think of a "classic" today, they don't think of a book, but a Coke, a 1950s roadster, or perhaps an early Beatles' song. Mark Twain defined the problem: a classic is a book that people praise, but don't read.

Why is it necessary for young adults to read the classics? Shouldn't only the dorks wearing flood pants read this stuff, while Christians spend our time loitering at Starbucks and listening to abecedarians on iTunes?

Huh?

According to Dr. Louise Cowan, we all are to read great books because,

They have been found to enhance and elevate the consciousness of all sorts of people who study them, to lift their readers out of narrowness or provincialism into a wider vision of humanity. Further, they guard the truths of the human heart from faddish half-truths of the day by straightening the mind and imagination and enabling their readers to judge for themselves. In a word, they lead those who will follow into a perception of the fullness and the complexity of reality.

Within a society that screams for us to pay attention to the minutiae and the immediate, foregoing contemplation upon the eternal and consequential, if the young adult doesn't want to be generational carnage, he must read things that are weighty, timeless, inspiring, and instructional.

The Wildman Devotional

As C.S. Lewis wrote:

We all, therefore, need the books that will correct the characteristic mistakes of our own period. And that means the old books ... the only palliative is to keep the clean sea breeze of the centuries blowing through our minds, and this can be done only by reading old books. It is a good rule, after reading a new book, never to allow yourself another new one till you have read an old one in between. If that is too much for you, you should at least read one old one to every three new ones.

THE WARFARE

Day 32

Hast Thou No Scar?

"And someone will say to him, 'What are these wounds between your arms?' Then he will say, 'Those with which I was wounded at the house of my friends.'"

– Zechariah 13:6 (NASB)

Here's a sermon you'll never hear at a youth group: Your "friends" and your family will probably screw you over.

Jesus' disciples abandoned Him (Mk 14:50). The Virgin Mary and His siblings thought that He was a nutjob (Mk 3:20-21). His homies from His hometown harangued Him (Mt 13:57-58).

Joseph's brothers crapped on him, selling him into slavery (Gen 37:18-36). Hello.

King David was also despised by his pusillanimous brothers and the envious people of God who lacked the gumption David had to kill Goliath (1Sam 17:28).

So ... if getting "wounded at the house of your friends" was par for the course for the biblical protagonists, you and I should not expect anything different.

When the animosity comes from "the house of your friends", here's three ways to roll with the punches and end up better and not some whiny, spiteful crank heaping scorn on everyone you see.

1. Blow off their putdowns and condescension. Who cares what they say or think if it goes against your calling and what God's word has declared you to be? Don't let them grind you down (Ps 3:6).

2. Don't stop serving God to attend to their blather. Jesus, Joseph, and David didn't get derailed by their friends' and family's digs at them. Plow forward and don't look back (Lk 9:62).

3. Don't get bitter, you little crybaby. If you don't forgive them, God won't forgive you (Mk 11:26). Make that a refrigerator magnet.

As noted, wounds are par for the course. If you don't have any then you probably ain't following God because everyone and their chihuahua in the scriptures who followed God fully got the shiitake mushrooms kicked out of them. Finally, and I'll shut

The Wildman Devotional

up now, by closing with this epic poem by Amy Carmichael that succinctly sums up this entry's biblical sentiment.

Hast thou no scar?

No hidden scar on foot, or side, or hand?

I hear thee sung as mighty in the land;

I hear them hail thy bright, ascendant star.

Hast thou no scar?

Hast thou no wound?

Yet I was wounded by the archers; spent,

Leaned Me against a tree to die; and rent

By ravening beasts that compassed Me, I swooned.

Hast thou no wound?

No wound? No scar?

Yet, as the Master shall the servant be,

And piercèd are the feet that follow Me.

But thine are whole; can he have followed far

Who hast no wound or scar?

Day 33

Trial ... You're A Friend Of Mine

"Consider it a sheer gift, friends, when tests and challenges come at you from all sides. You know that under pressure, your faith-life is forced into the open and shows its true colors. So don't try to get out of anything prematurely. Let it do its work so you become mature and well-developed, not deficient in any way."

– James 1:2-5 (MSG)

Was Jimmy high when he penned that nugget above?

Well, according to most bedazzled Charismatics, he had to be, because God, according to them, would not allow one of His dainty followers to go through some rancid test. Y'know ... some icky thing that would somehow taint their best life now?

In contrast, to the sputum spewed by the American Gospel Enterprise, the Bible uniformly states that the Christian will be stretched in life more than Rosie O'Donnell's yoga pants.

Instead of caterwauling when our gelatinous flesh gets pinched, James states the following ...

1. Consider (or regard, or deem, or declare, or view) the bullcrap that you're currently sloggin' through as a sheer gift from God. Especially, when the bovine scatology is hammering you from every conceivable angle. In other words, when some dipstick, smarmy, self-righteous, self-preening, religious peacock sees you mucking your way through a hellacious maelstrom and they ask you, "How are you doing?" Well, according to this text, you can full-throatedly say, "God's blessing me with a sick epic gift called pain! How you doin'?"

2. The reason James says to view this supposed negative as a positive is because this acid bath of pressure makes your faith real. It forces it out in the open to see if it is legit or not. It's easy to have faith when everything is peachy; it is a completely different thing to still believe when you're getting pummeled by Providence.

The Wildman Devotional

3. James advises the believer who's under duress to not attempt to find a quick fix and yet, that's what every Christian wants; namely a trial that only lasts about the same amount of time it takes to get your oil changed at Jiffy Lube.

4. Finally, James gives some eye salve to the battered believer that this frickin' mess they're momentarily mired in will not only prove their faith's mettle but will also make the Christian: A) Mature and not a solipsistic spiritual baby. B) Well-developed instead of a stunted Christian pygmy and C) A non-deficient disciple. Can you imagine God saying of you that you are mature, well-developed, and not deficient in any way? That would be quite the honor, eh? But y'know that type of divine accolade don't come easy, as Ringo Starr would say.

When I was going through one of my many ghoulish mosh pits, I penned this poem trying to make sense of it all. Check it out…

"Trial"

A testing,
A burning,
A place of despair.
A broken space,
Full of distress,
Where you alone are there.

Doug Giles

My friend you seem a foe of mine,
Unbecoming,
Distasteful,
Bitter wine,
But your intent and purpose is to prune the vine.

Trial...
You're a friend of mine

Day 34

Holy Adrenaline

"Do you see what this means—all these pioneers who blazed the way, all these veterans cheering us on? It means we'd better get on with it. Strip down, start running—and never quit! No extra spiritual fat, no parasitic sins. Keep your eyes on Jesus, who both began and finished this race we're in. Study how he did it. Because he never lost sight of where he was headed—that exhilarating finish in and with God—he could put up with anything along the way: Cross, shame, whatever. And now he's there, in the place of honor, right alongside God. When you find yourselves flagging in your faith, go over that story again, item by item, that long litany of hostility he plowed through. That will shoot adrenaline into your souls!"

– Hebrews 12:1-3 (MSG)

Did you know that Hebrews 11 precedes Hebrews 12?

I know ... you're thinking, "uh ... duh."

Well, forgive me for what seemed like a silly question, but you never know nowadays who went to public school and who did not. Anyway ...

What you might not know, if you're a typical lazy, biblically illiterate Christian is, Hebrews 11 features multiple mini-bios of epic men and women who kicked major demonic backside for God and His Kingdom concerns.

The reason the writer recounted these tremendous tales was to get you, the reader, to lather-rinse-and-repeat, similar heroic acts of faith and not be a useless Christian wuss. (That's the King Doug Translation of Hebrews 12:1).

The way we imitate these dang near inimitable protagonists, according to Peterson's rendering of Hebrews 12:1-3, is to do the following:

One. *Strip down, start running and never quit.* In other words, cowboy up Dinky (1Cor 16:13).

Two. *No spiritual fat or parasitic sins.* My translation? Quit wasting time and quit flirting with the spiritual poison from your past (Eph 5:11-19).

Three. *Keep your eyes on Jesus.* Here's five ditties on how to do that.

1. He began and ended His race. FYI: True

Christianity is a marathon (2Tim 4:8). It doesn't matter how many laps you lead if you don't finish the race.

2. Study how He did it. Forget how Buddha or Oprah did it. Study how Jesus did it (Eph 5:1).

3. He never lost sight of where He was headed. Jesus lived each day with the end in mind. Stay focused on His call and His will for your life and not Facebook's (Heb 10:7).

4. That caused Him to put up with a lot of garbage. Vision breeds tenacity. No vision, no tenacity (Mt 11:7).

5. When flagging in your faith, study the junk Jesus went through. It's great to study Jesus and others who went through way more poop than we have and they didn't curl up in the fetal position and wet their big Christian diapers (Heb 12:28).

So … what's the resultant effect of following the aforementioned exhortation? Well, according to Dr. Peterson, that'll *shoot adrenaline into your soul!*

I can't think of anything more needed in the body of Christ than for all of us to get a Holy Spirit-inspired, ten-thousand CC shot of a godly adrenaline jolt (Ps 69:9).

Day 35

Welcome To The Jungle

"Then Jesus was led up by the Spirit into the wilderness to be tempted by the devil."

– Matthew 4:1 (NASB)

Here's something that I wish ministers would tell their poor sheeple right after they get baptized: Dear So-and-So, now that you're a new creation in Christ Jesus you are now going to be attacked by the powers of darkness like cheap blouse marked down to $1.99 at Target's Black Friday Sale (1Pet 5:8,9).

Yes, boys and girls, once you say, "Yes!" to Jesus, Satan says, "to hell with you" and the temptations and demonic attacks come in like a flood.

Indeed, you're going to get tossed into a satanic woodchipper that's been chewing on saints since Adam and Eve got tossed out of the sweet haven of

Eden's crib (Gen 3).

Welcome to the Jungle.

It's time to nut up, shut up, and toughen up or you're not going to make it.

Look man, Jesus didn't have it easy (Jn 15). Why do you think you will?

Jesus waged war with the dragon and He did it with the Word of God.

Most typical Christians in today's easy-breezy, summer-squeezy churches are biblically illiterate and are thus no match for the malevolent one. When the powers of darkness tempt most believers to eat their plate of lies, they not only eat it, but they ask for seconds.

Serious Bible study is the stuff of men (Heb 5:12-14).

Tinkerpots don't read.

Tinkerpots don't think widely and deeply upon the Word of God.

Consequently, they're no match for the demonic hordes when it comes to the matching of wits and the ability to flee from Satan's multifaceted snares (Hos 4:6).

Jesus wasn't like that.

The Wildman Devotional

The word of God came thundering through His lips when Satan started yapping and therefore, He walked away The Victor instead of the victim of the devil's devices.

Oh, and I almost forgot, Jesus not only defeated Satan through the powerful wielding of God's holy word but he also did it on an empty stomach. Can you say, "Boom?"

Day 36

Satan Presents The Bait And Hides The Hook

"Satan disguises himself as an angel of light."

– 2Corinthians 11:14 (NASB)

Last November I had the pleasure of hunting whitetail deer on an epic spread in deep West Texas. The ranch hadn't been hunted in well over a decade. The place was teaming with whitetails, mule deer, turkeys, javelina, and loads of varmints. It was delicious.

The hunt coincided with the rut and I asked the landowner if we could try our hand at rattling up our bucks because I'd never personally done that before. I've seen it done lots of times on video but not in real life.

For those who're not hip to rattling, it's essentially trying to simulate two bucks fighting. Just like humans, deer love a good throwdown when their hormones are raging so they'll come in to see what's going on if the rattler is good at rattling. Our guide was great at it.

Our first setup brought in a main-frame eight-point mature buck to five yards right in front of us. It happened so fast that me and my buddy just stood there with our mouths open. We rattled in at least 20 bucks of various sizes and ages. It was way cool how we could deceive the deer into thinking the fight was real.

It's kinda like fishing where I present the bait and hide the hook. The fish crashes the bait thinking they happened upon a delicious *entre* only to find out it was a scam and they're now the *entre*. Similarly, the buck rushes to the fake fight thinking somebody is invading his turf or messing with his harem or both, only to be shot dead and get eaten by two Texas boys and their families.

Satan masquerades, folks. He cloaks himself. He pretends. He deceives. He feigns to be a good thing ... a veritable opportunity ... and the next thing you know you're in his trap.

To avoid getting clobbered by *el Diablo* do the following:

The Wildman Devotional

1. Stay close to God (Jn 15:1-9).

2. Drench yourself in the word (Ps 119:9).

3. Walk with serious believers (Acts 2:42) and …

4. Watch your six at all times. Satan plays for keeps. His goal is always to steal, kill and destroy (Jn 10:10).

5. Declare Christ's victory over Satan in your life (1Jn 2:14)!

Day 37

My Letter To The Devil

"Then he showed me Joshua the high priest standing before the angel of the Lord, and Satan standing at his right to accuse him."

– Zechariah 3:1 (NASB)

Satan's specialty is accusing Christians of their unworthiness to be loved or used by God.

Satan's also really good at pointing out a believer's past sins (Rev 12:10-12).

Matter of fact, other Christians are really good at doing both as well (Gal 5:15).

Let's settle this with Satan once and for all, shall we?

Dear Satan: FYI, *none* of us are worthy. Nobody has lived a squeaky-clean existence. All of mankind has veered severely off God's path. Our tongues spew forth garbage. Our hearts are full of lust, pride, and vanity and we have no desire or ability to stop that fetid course and yet, that's exactly the type of people Jesus came to save (Rom 3:9-25).

Therefore, *el Diablo*, when you accuse me/us of how unworthy we all are, we will use that accusation to warm the cockles of our heart because Christ died for and loves deeply the unworthy (1Cor 1:26-31).

Day 38

When Demons Try To Get You Down ... Do This

"Satan's angel did his best to get me down; what he in fact did was push me to my knees."

– 2Corinthians 12:7 (MSG)

As stated in this slim tome, and profusely throughout scripture, Satan is no fan of the on-fire believer (1Pet 5:8,9; Eph 6:10-20). The apostle Paul soared to heights in God that would give most Christians a violent nosebleed. Yep, Paul knew the Lord on a much higher level than your typical groovy youth pastor. With that high level of intimacy with God came a stack of devils that tried to wear Paul out.

What's weird is that God allowed Satan's vehement opposition to Paul to keep him from getting a big head.

The intense demonic opposition Paul went through didn't thrill Paul at all. Matter of fact, and as you can imagine, Paul begged God several times to get those evil monkeys off his back, and yet, our loving heavenly Father said, "No ... I like it when you are weak and dependent upon Me versus being a haughty-know-it-all-problem-free apostle." (Author's paraphrase)

When Paul got that download from the Lord he then saw all the garbage Satan was tossing in his direction as an actual gift that made him experience more of God's grace and His strength.

The demonic attacks which made Paul feel abused, opposed, hammered, and weak were morphed into more of God's divine favor and His holy supernatural strength toward Paul.

The resultant effect was that Paul now welcomed the warfare. He took getting opposed by *el Diablo* as an opportunity for Jesus to show Himself mighty in Paul's un-mightiness. Indeed, when Paul felt puny under Satan's assault that's when he became more powerful in Christ.

The Wildman Devotional

So my brothers, if Satan is wearing you out more than your little sister's first clarinet recital ever could, let hell's opposition drive you to your knees and watch God give you holy strength against Lucifer's unholy attacks.

Day 39

How To Quick Start Your Sad, Little Life

"Then said he unto the dresser of his vineyard, Behold, these three years I come seeking fruit on this fig tree, and find none: cut it down; why cumbereth it the ground? And he answering said unto him, Lord, let it alone this year also, till I shall dig about it, and dung it: And if it bear fruit, well: and if not, then after that thou shalt cut it down."

– Luke 13:7-9 (KJV)

Most people think that Jesus was/is some easy-going hippie who really doesn't care if we get a life or not.

The true Christ of the scripture expects fruit from His followers. Hello.

If we're in Christ, then we should be kicking butt and taking names in all areas of life.

Thus, if you are finding your life to be a tad lackluster and you've decided to rid your existence of as much suckiness as you can and you're finally ready for radical change; here are five sure-fire things that'll help you make a big leap forward in your walk with God.

1. Find Your Groove. What flicks your switch? If you could do whatever you wanted and it was righteous and somewhat feasible, what would you do? You have got to define your passion. Take the time to figure out what stirs your heart. Pinpoint it. Write it down and do it now. Don't play around. The epic peeps, hailed in scripture, weren't indecisive. John the Baptist didn't float from being a philosopher to an army man to a secret agent to a brain surgeon. John knew exactly what he was called to do, and he wouldn't mess with anything else.

Now granted, you might have a few side interests. That said, in order to kick butt in life, you've got jam to a solid, funky bottom-line bass note that is clear and unchanging. You must be able to spit out with absolute clarity what you are all about, what you live for, what you want from life . . . personally, familially, and vocationally. Define what you want, when

The Wildman Devotional

you want it, and in what quantity. If you don't, you will be a "woulda-shoulda-coulda" fruitless Christian the rest of your life.

To be continued ...

Day 40

How To Quick Start Your Sad, Little Life - Part 2

"But I keep under my body, and bring it into subjection: lest that by any means, when I have preached to others, I myself should be a castaway."

– 1 Corinthians 9:27 (KJV)

2. **Cut The Fat.** Fat will kill you. Fat is the excess baggage that is detrimental to your future progress. A good place to start is with the 50+ hours of TV/videos/games and social media you absorb each week. Get this into your brain: all that crap is an E.I.R.: Electronic Income Reducer. That stuff has killed more dreams and visions than crack

could ever hope to. If you intake any of that stuff, let it serve you instead of serving it. Watch it selectively. Watch TV/videos that push you into greatness. Watch and absorb what is noble and beneficial. (If you can find anything.) Use your time wisely.

Think about what a great path you could be on right now if instead of watching 50+ hours of that bullcrap you had utilized all those hours in developing your relationships with your kids, business, or personal growth. The longer your face stays buried in that tripe the longer you will remain a dolt. Anyway, who wants to sit for hours watching other people live out their desires while you drink warm beer on your titanium-reinforced, duct-taped La-Z-Boy in yo' mama's double wide trailer home?

Also, cut the fat on all non-productive relationships. Dad, quit hanging out with your going-nowhere buddies who resemble the cast of King of the Hill. Your kids miss you and need you.

Mom, don't let a messed up, gossiping, sexless, desperately-needs-to-get-a-life, soap-opera-watching, Facebook-devotee who eternally ties up your phone line and life rule your day.

Young person, don't hang around with a Satan-worshiping punk who wears Che Guevara t-shirts and has so many body piercings he looks like a tackle box blew up in his hands. You must also get away from kids who are always walking around holding their crotches, calling girls bad names, and using

The Wildman Devotional

their heads just to house dope smoke.

You must immediately get away from folks who want to remain morons.

As R.A. Dickinson said, "Love your enemies just in case your friends turn out to be a bunch of bastards."

I'm not being ugly for the sake of being ugly. I firmly believe in "loving thy neighbor" but choose your neighborhood. Get around people who have vision, great families, and a positive direction. Avoid being part of another person's carnage. If you simply took control of your TV/Social Media and separated from negative and smothering relationships, you would be well on your way to success.

To be continued …

Day 41

How To Quick Start Your Sad, Little Life - The Finale

"You've all been to the stadium and seen the athletes race. Everyone runs; one wins. Run to win. All good athletes train hard. They do it for a gold medal that tarnishes and fades. You're after one that's gold eternally."

– 1 Corinthians 9:24-25 (MSG)

3. **Change Your Crowd.** Since some of your friends and family members could be your greatest hindrances, you might have to make new relationships. But even if you don't have to end many of your current relationships, make yourself develop new ones. Add to the repertoire of people who affect your life. I have experienced incredible personal growth through hanging out with people

who aren't like me. Sure, it was initially uncomfortable; but the pain I temporarily went through with a new crowd was way less painful than hanging with the schleps with whom I used to run.

A car needs a battery that is charged by both a positive and a negative pole. Get around people who don't necessarily see things the same way you do, who have broader experiences than yours.

Don't inbreed, but synergize.

There are a lot of credible critters out there who can really challenge and enlighten you. Go find them, and you won't stay a putz for long.

4. **Set Killer Goals.** Outrageous, hard-to-reach targets will motivate you far more than reasonable ones. Never pick a small fight. In the Bible, David challenged and killed Goliath, not Goliath's ugly sister. What challenge is it for a Pitbull to whip a Rat Terrier?

Demand of yourself that which stretches you like a water-ski rope with a fat woman on the other end of it.

Don't measure your vision by what is reachable or by what other people are doing. Go for the "mission impossible." Incite people's ridicule, and use their derision to spur you on to greatness. Your success will be the sweetest revenge.

The Wildman Devotional

5. **Live Tooth, Fang, and Claw.** During your radical growth process, you must tattoo these four words on your soul: "I ain't gonna quit!" I know it's bad English, but you get the point. It took time to get into the mess you're in, and it'll take time to get out. Yet at the same time, don't be passive about being lackluster for Christ. Like Ted Nugent says, "Live tooth, fang, and claw." Aggressively attack the mirror. Work on your strengths until they've become stronger.

"Failure is only postponed success as long as courage 'coaches' ambition. The habit of persistence is the habit of victory."

– Herbert Kaufman

Lastly, if you've really blown it in the past, suck it up and move forward. Don't let your past kill your newfound Summit-or-Plummet Attitude. Take a good look over your right shoulder . . . then your left . . . and make that the last time you look back. From now on, you're more than a conqueror. Now go chase down your holy grail.

Day 42

Holy War

"Finally, be strong in the Lord and in the strength of His might. Put on the full armor of God, so that you will be able to stand firm against the schemes of the devil. For our struggle is not against flesh and blood, but against the rulers, against the powers, against the world forces of this darkness, against the spiritual forces of wickedness in the heavenly places."

– Ephesians 6:10-12 (NASB)

I was talking to a sister in Christ the other day and she was dismayed that a Christian that she looked up to had now renounced his faith and left his wife and kids. Her mentor had been a leader in a big church for many moons and now he's doing whoa-is-me pouty crap on IG saying stuff like, "There is no God and I hate him."

I know. Confusing, eh? Anyway …

Y'know, I wish the aforementioned apostate well. I truly do. I hope he gets his heart and mind settled in Christ again before he bounces off this mortal coil because the Judgment Seat will be rough on those who knew God and His word and blew Him and it off for whatever reason.

With that being said, I'd like to point out two things which Paul penned above in Ephesians 6:10-12.

1. **Satan has schemes against the Christian.** Yep, Dinky, *el Diablo* doesn't dig you and he and his demonic hordes are here to take you out. They constantly think of ways to ruin you and yours. Their craft is skullduggery, subterfuge, trickery, deception, dupery, and legerdemain and they're pretty adept at wielding those weapons. Please note that they've tripped up many of the scriptures' best and brightest boys and girls.

2. **Paul says not only are they stealthy with their wares but they're vehement in their opposition.** Paul says we struggle, or wrestle, with these unseen forces. Both of my daughters have black belts in Jujitsu and when I watch them roll it gets nasty. It gets violent. It is strenuous. Dealing with their opposition ain't pretty and that's exactly how Paul described our "walk with Jesus" as an epic war with a pissed-off dragon. A

The Wildman Devotional

war with powerful unseen demonic beings which requires we suit up in God's armor, be strong in His strength and stand firm against all of hell's henchmen and the bullcrap they throw our way. If not, Satan will clock us just like he did my friend's mentor.

This. Is. Not. A. Game.

Day 43

Stand Firm

"Therefore, take up the full armor of God, so that you will be able to resist on the evil day, and having done everything, to stand firm."

– Ephesians 6:13 (NASB)

The Apostle Paul effectively says, if you don't want to become roadkill under the wheel of Satan's Prius, you've got to do four things:

1. Take up the full armor of God.
2. Resist on the evil day.
3. Do everything necessary.
4. Stand firm.

Now, if what I just read is true, then the half-ass, capitulating, slack-jawed, wilting, and wussified evangelical world is screwed, glued, and tattooed because we are not what the Apostle ordered here in Ephesians 6.

The four traits Paul exhorts the believer to in Eph 6:13 states to this simple redneck that the demonic realm that we're up against is far more than we can handle on our own. We're in over our heads outside of Christ when it comes to matching wits and power with Satan and his ilk. Therefore, to be *laissez-faire* with the injunctions given by the Apostle Paul – who often danced with the devil – is to court our own ruination and that of our country and planet. *Capisce?*

Uh … earth to the Christian: you need all the help you can get in this eternal game against Lucifer.

In Christ, we've been saved by grace through faith. In Christ, we've been given a marvelous inheritance and we're God's adopted kids. In Christ, the chains that once enslaved us for years to various vices are shattered and He has guaranteed us eternal bliss via His resurrection from the dead. It's all yummy and that's a woefully incomplete list of what He's secured for the saint. That said, you and I won't experience any of that bliss if we're blissfully ignorant regarding the weapons of our warfare, if we're dilatory in their appropriation and if we bereft of defiance of the devil all the way to the bloody end.

I know … I know … it sucks. It sounds like a lot of hard and dirty work, and it is.

The Wildman Devotional

However, if we're prepped, if we're utilizing every epic weapon God has issued us, and if we're standing in the power of His might and not our own, then we get to see, in real-time, the crushing of Satan's devices underneath our feet. Yep, when the powers of darkness throw everything they have at us, the armored, diligent church gets to see the following fulfilled...

Rom 16:19b-20 *"...be wise in what is good, and innocent in what is evil. The God of peace will soon crush Satan under your feet."*

Day 44

Productive In Prison

"Are they servants of Christ? I am serving him more. (I am crazy to talk like this.) I have worked much harder than they. I have been in prison more often."

– 2Corinthians 11:23 (EXB)

In August of 2021 I caught COVID-19 for the second time. It wasn't too bad. It was worse than the first time but, again, it wasn't that devastating. However, it did knock me on my backside for a week.

While I was laying in bed with the Wuhan Wheezer, I started getting ticked off about this poison the Chinese unleashed on the planet and that my body wasn't running on all 8-cylinders. This rage against the Kung Flu and the idiots who created it and released it on the world actually inspired me, in my sick estate, to write a book.

The book I wrote that week, while demons and disease thought that they had me down, went on to be, at this writing, my #1 best-selling tome of all time. The book is, *Psalms of War: Prayers That Literally Kick Ass*.

I'm sure some of you are thinking, "dude … what's your point?"

Well, you inquiring mind, my point is: When bad crap happens to you, be it by design or default, turn it on its head and wring some good out of it.

I could've laid there and felt sorry for myself because I had the Chinese Sniffles, but I got pissed off and was productive instead.

I know a bro who had stage-four cancer. He went through brutal chemo treatments that lasted for months and months and during that excruciating, near death experience, he studied and earned a Ph.D. in Mandarin. Hello.

When the Apostle Paul got arrested do you know what he did? Well, he didn't waste his time feeling sorry for himself. What he did do was get busy writing to the church.

Indeed, I'm certain Satan and his defeated ilk thought they had Paul down for the count, but it was he that had them by the short and curlies. Can you say, "Boom?"

Yes, when demons thought they had shut Paul down in prison what they really did was give a chance to write eternal scripture that has punished demons for many, many moons. I have one word for that: Ahahahahahahahahahahahahaha!

Four Holy Ghost-inspired letters, that include Ephesians, Philippians, Colossians, and Philemon rose out of Pablo's time in the pokey. The contents of those Prison Epistles include epic treatments of salvation by grace through faith alone (Eph 2:1-10), the Christian way of life (Eph 4-5) and our victorious warfare against *el Diablo* (Eph 6:10-18).

Accordingly, my brothers, please understand when it looks like Satan or some man-made bullcrap has got you cornered and conquered, remember that Jesus is still Lord of All. Satan always overplays his hand. Ask God to show you His will and way when your current local condition sucks and watch what He does through your life and make the Malevolent One sorry he ever messed with you.

Day 45

You Can't "Love Jesus" And Not Feast On His Word

"It takes more than bread to stay alive. It takes a steady stream of words from God's mouth."

– Matthew 4:4 (MSG)

I've been a Christian, as of July 4th, 2022, for thirty-nine years. During that time frame I've heard more than once guys and gals say stupid stuff like, "I love Jesus, but I'm not really into theology and stuff."

Uh … okay.

So, what you're actually saying is, "You love Jesus but definitive definitions, in the sacred scripture, regarding His nature and character; His person, words, and works are a bridge too far for your persnickety palette?"

The scary thing about that mindset is not only how outlandishly stupid it is but some people think that the abecedarians who spew such sputum are somehow, "more spiritual" than those po' rubes who take theology seriously.

How can someone "love Jesus" and not have a high view of scripture?

That's hogwash.

That's nonsense.

That's something Satan would say.

Jesus said to the Devil, while duking it out with him in the wilderness, that "Man shall not live on bread alone, but on every word that comes out of the mouth of God." (Mt 4:4)

Jesus put the word of God in the food category, folks. It's essential to the believer. And that would be every word that tumbled out of God's mouth, not just the ones we pick and chose.

The only way we know the true Christ of the scripture is through theology furnished by the word of God. People who ignore or stray from the *Verbum Dei* are tofu for deceiving spirits and doctrines of demons. They have no holy sword of the Spirit to fend off Satan's slick lies and are a piece of cake for demonic deception, fo' sho'.

If I were you, I'd run from the tripe that claims someone can love Jesus and not be in love with His Word. He is the Word. Hello. If you don't believe me Google John 1:1.

Finally, enjoy this quote from my former professor and Christian heavy-weight, Dr. R.C. Sproul, "There is an inseparable relationship between your affection for Christ and your affection for the scripture."

Send that Sproul quote over to the doe-eyed, miscreant, "Christian" zombies that you know who currently think contrary to that quote. It could save their soul ...

Day 46

Revival From The Pit

"You have made me see hard times: I've experienced many miserable days, but You will restore me again. You will raise me up from the deep pit."

— Psalm 71:20 (VOICE)

Here's some stuff that you won't hear at Light-A-Fart Community Church's "Youth Group": godly people, even God's favorites, will see hard times and experience many miserable days. They'll tumble into a "deep pit".

That's a fact, Jack.

Yes, I know it's contrary to what your typical grin-until-your-teeth-are-dried Pastor Feelgood will tell you, but the examples, in the scripture, of holy folks going through holy hell, are replete (Heb 11).

King David didn't have a smooth walk in the park when he strode this blue marble 3000 years ago. Oh, no *senorita*.

David even said, "You (God) have made me see hard times."

Most American Christians would say, "Man that ain't fair. No wonder why God has so few friends nowadays."

Y'know what? I can't relate with "problem-free people". Not at all.

I have a lot of problems. Problems that I create, that my sin nature spawns, and that demons tempt me into. Aside from that, I have trials that challenge my calling, Christ's Church, my family, our culture, and this great Nation. There's frickin' trouble aplenty on my plate on a regular basis.

Our story and David's story does not end with just problems galore. David said of God, that the Lord restores, revives, and raises those who're going through life's woodchipper. God doesn't just let us linger through rough times and misery. He's a God of revival. He's a God of resurrection. He's a God of restoration and when He restores it's always greater in quality, quantity, and kind.

Currently, while I type this slim tome to you, the reader, I'm going through some unpleasant bull hockey. It is not fun. I do not like it at all. It's confusing and depressing and I would despair if I did not know God is a God who restores and will raise me up again.

The Wildman Devotional

If you're currently getting the stuffing kicked out of you, cling to the promise of Ps 71:20 like grim death. Declare it out loud. Declare it in faith. Declare it with great boldness.

If you're currently not going through a bunch of bollocks and your glide path is pretty pleasant and turbulence-free, file this scripture away because hard times and misery will hit everyone eventually and you'll need this golden nugget one day.

Day 47

Who's Training You?

"Blessed be the Lord, my rock, Who trains my hands for war, And my fingers for battle"

– Psalm 144:1 (NASB)

When I was a teen, baseball was my sport. I loved it and excelled at playing it until I became a drug-addled moron.

Looking back on those baseball years, I can remember only one coach who really upped my game. The other coaches were more like gruff, unfocused baby-sitters or hairy youth pastors, but coach John ... well ... he greatly honed my pitching and hitting skills. Under his tutelage, I made it to the All Stars that year as the starting pitcher and I batted first in the line-up. Ah, the good ol' glory days. Do I sound like Uncle Rico, or what?

Anyway ...

With a good trainer/coach great things can be accomplished with our natural gifts and spiritual bents. My walk with God has benefited greatly via the pastors, mentors, authors, professors, and solid brothers and sisters that God has blessed me with over the last forty years. They prepared me for life. They prepared me for battle. It's been an insane blessing to have had these great people sow into my life.

King David, on the other hand, didn't have the litany of leaders that I have to help hone his craft. There's zero mention of his old man fussing over David's life. The only thing King Saul wanted to do for David was to let the air out of his lungs and kill him. Samuel was kind of a hit-and-run relationship. And Nathan didn't show up in David's world until he was a grown man. Yep, David was a loner, but he was not alone, and he was not without assistance. God was there to coach David through the dicey days which made up his entire existence.

David learned warfare from The Master. I'm talking about God Himself.

Can you imagine having God be your personal trainer? He knows your gifts, proclivities, and the funky bottom-line bass note that makes you rattle and hum. In addition, He's well-aware of your spiritual gifts because He gave them to you.

Also, can you imagine how slighted God must feel when His people run off to Tony Robbins to be coached and trained instead of seeking The Ultimate Trainer's training?

I think our lives and the church would look a whole lot different if an all-knowing and a very creative God coached and trained us instead of mommy and daddy, dead churches, fearful parents, and a me-monkey culture.

The Wildman Devotional

Imagine if God were to coach you how to …

- Preach and teach.

- Reach lost souls.

- Paint, play music, write, and make sculptures.

- Give of your finances.

- Serve His body and your community.

- Invest your time, talent, and treasure.

- Run your business.

- Lead your family.

If God coached us, I guarantee it would not be boring. Our lives would not be cookie-cutters of conformity. Our time here on this third rock from the sun would be one of holy significance.

David's life didn't suck. David left a scar on this planet, and it can all be traced back to this one little phrase … God trained his hands for war.

Y'know, it's great to have awesome men and women of God in one's life. It's also great to have Jehovah as your Ultimate Head Coach. Go to God today and ask Him to train you for spiritual warfare like He did David. Make some time today to have an epic one-on-one session with The Warrior of Warriors. You won't regret it.

Day 48

Rider On A White Horse

"And I saw heaven opened, and behold, a white horse, and He who sat on it is called Faithful and True, and in righteousness He judges and wages war. His eyes are a flame of fire, and on His head are many diadems; and He has a name written on Him which no one knows except Himself. He is clothed with a robe dipped in blood, and His name is called The Word of God. And the armies which are in heaven, clothed in fine linen, white and clean, were following Him on white horses. From His mouth comes a sharp sword, so that with it He may strike down the nations, and He will rule them with a rod of iron; and He treads the wine press of the fierce wrath of God, the Almighty. And on His robe and on His thigh He has a name written, 'KING OF KINGS, AND LORD OF LORDS.'"

– Revelation 19:11-16 (NASB)

When the misinformed thinks of Jesus nowadays, one imagines ...

An overly ebullient, grinning hick with a curly mullet, a man bag, and a quaint southern drawl, who spits out more aphorisms than Joel Osteen on crystal-meth-laced Mountain Dew.

Or The Nazarene gets painted as some rambling, Rasputin-like mystic who strings together long, illogical stories like an unshorn, Bruce Banner-inspired, Matthew McConaughey grad speech.

Either that or Jesus Christo gets pitched as some unisexual, religious, gluten-free Gucci model who might confuse us in regards to his actual gender, but he's crystal clear with his message that we should all be tolerant of the ridiculous no matter how much it offends reason.

Two things are for certain in our culture's postmodern paranormal messaging regarding Christ and Christians:

Jesus is not a warrior and ... Christianity is for wimps

Indeed, our wussified culture has created for themselves a wussified, Faux Christ, who's nicer than the actual Jesus and has little to nothing to do with the rebellious, young Galilean who jettisoned evil politicians and priests and crushed *el Diablo* two thousand years ago.

The Wildman Devotional

Consequently, his followers are expected to produce gelded disciples who do not upset the world like the first century believers did.

Well, as you can imagine, Dear Reader, I'm here to blow that nonsense all to smithereens.

The Jesus revealed to John in the Book of Revelation (in the first-century mind you) was not a sweet religious bearded lady doling out daisies and riddles. Oh, heck no.

Let's go through the list of how John described Jesus in His ascended state, shall we?

1. First of all, He's no punk deity. I got that right off the bat reading that chunk of text. Did you? He, Jesus, is King of Kings and Lord of Lords. Satan's not the power broker. Jesus is. Please note that.

2. Lawlessness is in Christ's crosshairs. According to the text, Jesus is currently warring in pure righteousness against evil.

3. Via the sharp sword that comes out of His mouth He, not the Devil, will subdue and rule nations through the power of the gospel.

4. He will tread on God's enemies in the great winepress of the wrath of God.

Question: does the aforementioned elevate the picture of the Lord whom you serve? It does to me.

The apostle Paul knew *that* Jesus. That's why he could say with great boldness ...

So, what do you think? With God on our side like this, how can we lose? If God didn't hesitate to put everything on the line for us, embracing our condition and exposing himself to the worst by sending his own Son, is there anything else he wouldn't gladly and freely do for us? And who would dare tangle with God by messing with one of God's chosen? Who would dare even to point a finger? The One who died for us – who was raised to life for us – is in the presence of God at this very moment sticking up for us. Do you think anyone is going to be able to drive a wedge between us and Christ's love for us? There is no way! Not trouble, not hard times, not hatred, not hunger, not homelessness, not bullying threats, not backstabbing, not even the worst sins listed in Scripture:

They kill us in cold blood because they hate you.

We're sitting ducks; they pick us off one by one.

None of this fazes us because Jesus loves us. I'm absolutely convinced that nothing—nothing living or dead, angelic or demonic, today or tomorrow, high or low, thinkable or unthinkable—absolutely *nothing* can get between us and God's love because of the way that Jesus our Master has embraced us. (Rom 8:31-39)

Day 49

Spiritual Violence

I've been asked by believers, "What is my favorite scripture?" My answer is, "Uh … all of them." I don't have favorite kids or grandkids. I love them all just like I do the whole enchilada of the *Verbum Dei*. That said, when I do sign my books at events, if I do add a scripture reference with my John Hancock, it is usually Matthew 11:12. For those of you who are not hip to Matthew 11:12 (NKJV) here it is …

> *"From the days of John the Baptist until now the kingdom of heaven suffers violence, and violent men take it by force."*

Let's dig into this little biblical nugget, shall we?

Here's an FYI: When John The Baptist rocked up on the scene, as the emcee of history's main event, he was a holy wrecking crane to dead religion and evil politicians.

For four hundred years there was no prophetic word going forth.

God wasn't saying squat.

Until John.

And when John opened his mouth, he shook all of hell.

John was a rowdy equal-opportunity offender and boy howdy ... was John good at his job.

John, like Jesus, was not some little Twinkie.

When John preached, you wouldn't go to sleep while he spoke.

When John preached, you wouldn't wonder what he meant.

John left blisters on his listeners' souls.

John spawned conflict everywhere he went.

Where John trod, he left a combination of riots and revival in his wake.

I bet today's pastoral search committees would "pass" on asking John to pastor their Church because that brother generated nothing but solid angst wherever he went.

That first-century *amigo*, with his call to repentance, stirred up devils in every corridor of hell to such an extent that the only way to shut him down was to cut off his head.

The Wildman Devotional

And that's exactly what they did.

Jesus, in light of John's hell-razing ministry, said in effect, if you want to get in on what God's doing now, you're going to have to get and stay, spiritually scrappy.

The Kingdom of God brings conflict and unless we're "spiritually violent" we're going to be roadkill under the wheels of satanic attacks.

John and Jesus were verbally attacked, physically assaulted, and both were ultimately murdered for The Message.

Half-hearted commitments to Christ won't suffice ever since John opened up his glorious mouth and let the devils have it.

The Amplified Bible puts Matthew 11:12 this way ...

> *"And from the days of John the Baptist until the present time, the kingdom of heaven has endured violent assault, and violent men seize it by force (as a precious prize – a share in the heavenly kingdom is sought with most ardent zeal and intense exertion)."*

Did you catch what Jesus said was the violent attitude needed for one to "share in the heavenly kingdom?" You have to see being on Jesus' team as a "precious prize" that requires a "most ardent zeal" and "intense devotion". And there went 90% of folks who claim Christ.

Question: How many Christians can you name who value Jesus and His kingdom as a "precious prize?" Not precious in the "aww, isn't that cute" sense of the word, but that which is highly valuable and is esteemed above every other person or thing or aspiration this planet has to offer?

Paul valued the person and work of Christ like that. Check it out in Philippians 3:7,8

> *"But whatever things were gain to me, those things I have counted as loss for the sake of Christ. More than that, I count all things to be loss in view of the surpassing value of knowing Christ Jesus my Lord, or whom I have suffered the loss of all things, and count them but rubbish so that I may gain Christ ..."*

Paul's affections ran hot for God. He did "violence" to everything that tried to seduce him away from the Father and His will. Yep, whether it was his lower cortex, me-monkey, carnal appetites or his self-righteous religious pedigree, anything that would tempt him away from Christ and Christ alone got the Pauline woodchipper.

Question number two: How many Christian folks do you know who sport a "most ardent zeal" and "intense devotion?" Who can be characterized as having an extreme, passionate, energetic pursuit of the things of God that is unrelenting in force, degree, and strength in their love and loyalty to Jesus and The Gospel?

The Wildman Devotional

This is what Jesus calls, "'violence". The person who has this is the one who gets "a share in His heavenly kingdom."

Make us "violent", Lord.

Day 50

My Testimony

"Let the redeemed of the Lord say so, whom he hath redeemed from the hand of the enemy."

– Psalm 107:2 (KJV)

Here's my personal testimony. I didn't go to a church until I got converted at the age of twenty-one. My parents weren't drug dealers or sex traffickers, they just didn't claim to be Christians, so they didn't pretend to be by going to church. And you know what? I appreciate that.

Yep, we didn't go to church at all. Not on Easter or Christmas. I'm talking about no immediate church experience for me. Not even weddings or funerals. Indeed, there were zero *kumbaya* gatherings for this Cretin.

What I knew about Christians was primarily via

the guys and gals I bumped up against in high school.

What I gained from my interactions with the Christian males I ran into was this: they're self-righteous softies who wanted me to go to hell. Suffice it to say, we didn't get along at all and becoming a Christian was not on my "To Do" list.

But God had other plans ...

From the age of thirteen to twenty-one, I was hell on two skinny legs. I started drinking pretty heavily and regularly at thirteen and around sixteen I saw *Fast Times At Ridgemont High* and started taking notes. By the end of that year, I was dealing weed, LSD, and speed.

I was an evil little monster. I was not a good person. Not at all.

All I wanted was sex, a solid buzz, a fast car ... and that was it. I kept it simple because I was stupid.

Please note: I was not on a spiritual quest. I did not want to be a Christian and I heartily expected that if I died, my elevator would not be going up. I was going straight to hell. I was under no delusions about "being a good boy, who meant well, but was troubled." I knew I was damned and honestly; I was okay with that ... for a while.

I won't bore you with the details, but God had my number and I started feeling "weird" when I would do bad crap beginning around the age of eighteen and, heretofore, I had never felt bad. It was all a big joke to me.

The Wildman Devotional

Around 1981 that callousness began to erode.

At that stage of the game, I was way down the funnel of evil and it wasn't funny anymore and people were being hurt and I was getting arrested.

The stakes were high and so was I.

I knew I needed a change, but I did not want to start going to church because most of the Christian males I met in high school were wussies and I didn't not want to be a wussy.

So, instead of becoming a choir boy, I started dialing back on my partying and started working out. "Exercise versus excess", I thought. That was my solution to my current level of pollution which wasn't totally bad, mind you.

It was, however, short-lived. My conscience was still kicking my butt. The working out wasn't drowning out the guilt I had for what I had done and who I knew I was at my core namely, a sinner. *Ergo*, I did what any good sinner would do and cranked back up the drinking, sex, and drug machine to silence "the voices".

My next three years were really bad. I don't even remember most of them. Just lots of booze, weed, acid, and cocaine.

I'll never forget one night, me and my buddy Joe were cooking on some blotter, hanging out at a closed public pool, just tripping away and talking about ... God?

Yep, we were talking about God. Wondering if

He existed and if there was a right and wrong and how, if there was the aforementioned, and we had to meet Him, then man oh, man; were we on the wrong side of that equation. But still, nothing of substance changed in me.

It was at that juncture, when I was finally entertaining God, righteousness, death, and judgment that I started getting bombarded with thoughts from my evil angels saying, "You don't want to be a Christian. Christians are wussies. People will mock you. Who wants to be that?" And like an idiot, I believed that low-level devil and I carried on in my self-destructive course, blowing off God and indulging deeply in what Saint James called, "the superfluity of naughtiness". That was until December 7th, 1983. On that fateful night God poleaxed me.

Here's how it went down.

My dad and I were watching *NBC Nightly News* with Tom Brokaw and Tom was talking about a fourteen-year-old kid who'd just graduated college. I was twenty-one years old and had just been kicked out of college and Brokaw's little vignette on this over-achiever made me feel like *Beavis & Butthead* on steroids. I felt like I should've felt: like a loser. My dad didn't say a word but I knew what he was thinking namely, "when is he going to get his act together?"

Following my normal course of action after getting convicted of my sin, I went and got my girlfriend at Texas Tech, my weed stash, and a 12-pack of Silver Bullets, and off we went to get high and bump uglies.

The Wildman Devotional

While we were partying in my car, out of nowhere, I told my main squeeze that I wanted to go home. She's like, "We just got here. What's wrong?" I said, nothing and that I just want to go home. She said ok and off we went, back home in the middle of our "date."

When I got back to my house my girlfriend and I got into an argument that got pretty heated out in front of my house. It was so loud that my dad and brother came outside to see what the heck was going on. When my dad stepped off the porch and started heading towards me in the driveway I ran towards him, embraced him, and asked him to forgive me for all the horrible crap I'd done to him and mom. I collapsed. I wept. Everyone was like, "Whiskey. Tango. Foxtrot!" Where did this come from? I was broken. I was shattered. The game was over.

After I'd calmed down a bit, my girlfriend and I loaded back up in my car, and off we went to drop her off at her dorm. However, we didn't get very far. It started hitting me again. Namely, a massive sense of guilt and conviction. It was so bad that I had to pull my vehicle over in an apartment parking lot. My girl's really freaking now. "What's wrong? What's happening to you?" she asked. All I could do was weep. And I mean capital W-E-E-P, weep. Finally, out from under the massive flow of tears and phlegm, I said to God, not to her, "God if you're real and if Jesus is who people say he is then please change me." And boom. It happened.

On December 7th, 1983, I got converted and it was radical and ugly. Immediately I stopped the drugs and the booze abuse. I no longer wanted it. I wanted God instead. My former vices no longer appealed to me. All I wanted to do was pursue the God who pursued me, the clod.

Now, in case you missed it, let me reiterate what was a major sticking point to my aversion to becoming a Christian. It was something that the powers of darkness really used against me, the rebel without a clue. It was this – if I became a Christian, based on what I saw and heard from Christians in high school, that means that I would have to become a wussy and becoming a wussy appeared nowhere on my Christmas wish list.

For example, I experienced major, and I mean major conviction, and yet I didn't want to become a Christian because of the effeminized Christian males I'd met. I was almost bargaining with God. It went something like this, "Please forgive me, let me go to heaven, but don't make me sing sappy songs, wear nerdy 'Christian' clothes and act like Jim Bakker on The PTL Club, or like that lame dork named, Todd, the Youth Group director."

I kid you not.

I wanted to be forgiven but I did not want to become a "Christian".

Again, from what I'd gathered from interacting with male, high school Christians, was that Jesus and church attendance gelds a guy and gelded I did not want to get.

These were real problems to me as a young Turk

The Wildman Devotional

who'd grown up watching the likes of Clint Eastwood, John Wayne, Steve McQueen, The Dallas Cowboys, and being around WWII adults.

Yes, my lofty aspirations, when I actually had some, were to kill dragons, save nations, and throttle some enemy with a Raquel Welch clone at my side. Wearing a cardigan and singing *I'll Fly Away* while holding hands with other men as we talk about our feelings and how wrong it is to masturbate was nightmarish to me.

It was not cool.

It was not inspiring. It was not masculine.

And I wanted, more than anything, as a lost man, to be masculine. As all boys do. Aside from Bruce Jenner, of course. But my sins had become too much for me to bear and I caved. God won. I got converted and a couple of months later I finally went to church. And you know what? All my suspicions were spot on. It was very effeminate.

Mind you, and pardon my redundancy, I had no knowledge base about what went down in church having never, ever, been before. I just knew what I knew about believers from high school and seeing the scary peeps on The PTL Club at my aunt's house when we would visit. I came in raw, and I'll never forget my first blush with the brethren. Never. All my fears were spot on. The Church, by and large, had been severely effeminized.

Thank God I met some bros who loved God and didn't like to knit but liked to hunt and fish instead.

I also met some epic dudes who loved God wholeheartedly and liked to debate and do jail, street, bar, and rock concert ministry and radical missions way down deep in Mexican jungles.

Look folks, God hardwired men, in His image, to be providers, protectors, hunters, and heroes under His governance. For pastors or anyone else to try to effeminize the *Imago Dei* and foist that lie upon men's psyche, is to bastardize the scripture, deceive men into denying their God-given masculine traits, and to me, that ranks up there with the Unpardonable Sin.

About the Author

Doug earned his Bachelor of Fine Arts degree from Texas Tech University and his certificates in both Theological and Biblical Studies from Knox Theological Seminary (Dr. D. James Kennedy, Chancellor). Giles was fortunate to have Dr. R.C. Sproul as an instructor for many classes.

Doug Giles is the host of The Doug Giles Podcast, the co-founder and co-host of the Warriors & Wildmen podcast (1M+ downloads) and the man behind ClashDaily.com. In addition to driving ClashDaily.com (290M+ page views), Giles is the author of several #1 Amazon bestsellers. His book *Psalms of War: Prayers That Literally Kick Ass* (2021) spent 26 weeks at #1 on Amazon. In 2018, Giles was permanently banned from his two-million followers on Facebook.

Doug is also an artist and a filmmaker and his online gallery can be seen at DougGiles.Art. His first film, *Biblical Badasses: A Raw Look at Christianity and Art*, is available via DougGiles.Art.

Doug's writings have appeared in several other print and online news sources, including Townhall.com, The Washington Times, The Daily Caller, Fox Nation, Human Events, USA Today, The Wall Street Journal, The Washington Examiner, American Hunter Magazine, and ABC News.

Giles and his wife Margaret have two daughters, Hannah and Regis. Hannah devastated ACORN with her 2009 nation-shaking undercover videos and she currently stars in the explosive 2018 Tribeca Documentary, Acorn and The Firestorm.

Regis has been featured in Elle, American Hunter, and Variety magazines. Regis is also the author of a powerful book titled, *How Not To Be A #Me-Too Victim, But A #WarriorChick*.

Regis and Hannah are both black belts in Gracie/Valente Jiu-Jitsu.

The Wildman Devotional

Speaking Engagements

Doug Giles speaks to college, business, community, church, advocacy and men's groups throughout the United States and internationally. His expertise includes issues of Christianity and culture, masculinity vs. wussification, God and government, big game hunting and fishing, raising righteous kids in a rank culture, the Second Amendment, personal empowerment, and social change. To invite Doug to speak at your next event, log on to DougGiles.org and fill out the invitation request.

Doug Giles

Accolades for Giles include ...

– *Giles was recognized as one of "The 50 Best Conservative Columnists Of 2015"*

– *Giles was recognized as one of "The 50 Best Conservative Columnists Of 2014"*

– *Giles was recognized as one of "The 50 Best Conservative Columnists Of 2013"*

– *ClashDaily.com was recognized as one of "The 100 Most Popular Conservative Websites For 2013 and 2020"*

– *Doug was noted as "Hot Conservative New Media Superman" By Politichicks*

Between 2002 – 2006, Doug's 3-minute daily commentary in Miami received seven Silver Microphone Awards and two Communicator Awards.

The Wildman Devotional

Doug's podcast can be seen and heard at
ClashRadio.com.

Doug Giles

Books by Doug Giles

Dear Christian: Your Fear Is Full of Crap

Psalms of War: Prayers That Literally Kick Ass

Biblical Badasses: The Women

If Masculinity is 'Toxic,' Call Jesus Radioactive

Would Jesus Vote For Trump?

Rules For Radical Christians: 10 Biblical Disciplines for Influential Believers

Pussification: The Effeminization Of The American Male

Raising Righteous And Rowdy Girls

Raising Boys Feminists Will Hate

Rise, Kill and Eat: A Theology of Hunting From Genesis to Revelation.

If You're Going Through Hell, Keep Going

My Grandpa is a Patriotic Badass

A Coloring Book for College Cry Babies

Sandy Hook Massacre: When Seconds Count, Police Are Minutes Away

The Bulldog Attitude: Get It or ... Get Left Behind

A Time To Clash

10 Habits of Decidedly Defective People: The Successful Loser's Guide to Life

Political Twerps, Cultural Jerks, Church Quirks

The Wildman Devotional

Theologians call these specific prayers, from the psalmist David, "imprecatory prayers." They are prayers to pull out and pray when things get bad – as in real bad. Prayers you use when a nation's getting mucked up by degenerate priests or politicians, or when the enemy is crushing the people of God, or when your flesh/personal demons are out of control.

King David was the king of this type of incendiary intercession. This giant killer slayed more Goliaths in his prayers and songs than he ever did with a rock and slingshot. Oh, and by the way, Jesus said all those imprecations David dealt out were not the mad ramblings of a ticked off warrior poet, but were actually inspired by the Holy Spirit. (See Matthew 22:43.)

Psalms of War: Prayers That Literally Kick Ass is a compendium from the book of Psalms, regarding how David rolled in prayer. I bet you haven't heard these read, prayed or sang in church against our formidable enemies, have you? I didn't think so. It might be time to dust them off and offer 'em up if you're truly concerned about the state of Christ's Church and our nation.

Also included in this book, *Psalms of War*, are full-color reproductions of the author's original art from his Biblical Badass Series of oil paintings.

Made in the USA
Middletown, DE
09 November 2022